THE SEMIOTICS
OF EMOJI

BLOOMSBURY ADVANCES IN SEMIOTICS

Semiotics has complemented linguistics by expanding its scope beyond the phoneme and the sentence to include texts and discourse, and their rhetorical, performative, and ideological functions. It has brought into focus the multimodality of human communication. *Advances in Semiotics* publishes original works in the field demonstrating robust scholarship, intellectual creativity, and clarity of exposition. These works apply semiotic approaches to linguistics and nonverbal productions, social institutions and discourses, embodied cognition and communication, and the new virtual realities that have been ushered in by the Internet. It also is inclusive of publications in relevant domains such as socio-semiotics, evolutionary semiotics, game theory, cultural and literary studies, human-computer interactions, and the challenging new dimensions of human networking afforded by social websites.

Series Editor: Paul Bouissac is Professor Emeritus at the University of Toronto (Victoria College), Canada. He is a world renowned figure in semiotics and a pioneer of circus studies. He runs the SemiotiX Bulletin [www.semioticon.com/semiotix] which has a global readership.

Titles in the Series:

THE SEMIOTICS OF EMOJI

Marcel Danesi

Bloomsbury Academic
An imprint of Bloomsbury Publishing Plc

B L O O M S B U R Y
LONDON · OXFORD · NEW YORK · NEW DELHI · SYDNEY

Bloomsbury Academic
An imprint of Bloomsbury Publishing Plc

50 Bedford Square
London
WC1B 3DP
UK

1385 Broadway
New York
NY 10018
USA

www.bloomsbury.com

**BLOOMSBURY and the Diana logo are trademarks
of Bloomsbury Publishing Plc**

First published 2017

British Library Cataloguing-in-Publication Data
A catalogue record for this book is available from the British Library.

ISBN: HB: 978-1-4742-8199-7
PB: 978-1-4742-8198-0
ePDF: 978-1-4742-8201-7
ePub: 978-1-4742-8200-0

Library of Congress Cataloging-in-Publication Data
A catalog record for this book is available from the Library of Congress.

Series: Bloomsbury Advances in Semiotics

Typeset by Deanta Global Publishing Services, Chennai, India
Printed and bound in Great Britain

CONTENTS

PREFACE

The world doesn't make sense, so why should I paint pictures that do?
PABLO PICASSO (1881–1973)

In 2015, a truly remarkable event occurred. The emoji known as "Face with Tears of Joy," 😂, was chosen by the Oxford Dictionary as the "*Word* of the Year." Not only was it not a word—it was a pictogram—but it was chosen by one of the most prestigious dictionaries in the world. Incredibly, the choice did not garner any significant complaints, protests, or polemical arguments from the guardians of traditional literacy (academics, teachers, language purists, and so on). This was a mind-boggling event in many ways, signaling that a veritable paradigm shift might have taken place in human communications and even human consciousness.

On its website, the Oxford Dictionary explained that it chose a pictogram over a word because it "captures the ethos, mood, and preoccupations" of the year and reflects "the sharp increase in popularity of emoji across the world in 2015." Is this increase a signal that print-based literacy is declining since the arrival of Web 2.0 technologies? The spread of literacy is traced to the invention of moveable print technology in the late 1400s, which made printed materials broadly available and inexpensive, encouraging the acquisition of literacy among all classes of people. But the same kind of literacy that has served us so well since at least the sixteenth century may have, over the last few decades, lost much of its social value and prestige, as the Oxford Dictionary choice subconsciously suggested. The Internet Age is making new kinds of demands on writing practices, relegating the traditional practices increasingly to the margins.

The Internet has brought about new forms of writing and literacy. According to research carried out by Oxford University Press and the mobile technology business, SwiftKey, the "Face with Tears of Joy" made up over 20 percent of all emoji used in Britain in 2015, and 17 percent of all emoji used in the United States. Emoji are, in fact, becoming increasingly popular across the world, allowing people from different linguistic and cultural backgrounds to communicate and interact with each other more concretely, thus making it possible to facilitate intercultural communications by transcending the symbolic barriers of the past demarcated by specific scripts and the implicit sociopolitical ideologies that they entailed. In the current age of "connected global intelligence" these may have started collapsing.

This book is an attempt to explain why the topic of emoji is a significant one for everyone. In the age of the "electronic global village" where people of different national languages and cultures are in frequent contact through online interactions, the emoji code might well be the universal language that can help solve problems of comprehension that international communications have always involved in the past. Used initially in Japanese electronic messages and Web pages, but now used by anyone, irrespective of language or cultural background, the emoji code harbors within it many implications for the future of writing, literacy, and even human consciousness. Recalling movements, such as the Blissymbolic one which was proposed as an alternative to the vagaries and variability of phonetic writing systems, the emoji code may well be an indication of how writing and literacy are evolving; on the other hand, emoji may just be a passing fad. Either way, the study of the emoji phenomenon is, clearly, a rather significant one.

This book will look at emoji primarily from a semiotic perspective, adopting a nontechnical style, so that a general audience can engage with its subject matter. I will focus on emoji as signs or symbols connected to each other in specific semiotic (meaning-making) and formal ways, without utilizing the technical lexicon and often intricate notions of theoretical semiotics. However, I will not completely skirt around all technical matters, since this would water down my treatment considerably. However, if a specific technical notion is required at some point, I will define it or illustrate it as concretely as possible. Nothing is taken for granted in this book.

Many of the analyses carried out and described here are based on a database compiled at the University of Toronto, consisting of electronic messages that involve the use of emoji. The information for the database was collected by a "research team" of four students at the university— Nadia Guarino, Soli Doubash, Lily Che, and Yvone Tuan. They were assigned two main tasks: (1) collect actual written materials that allow for a first-hand analysis of emoji, and (2) interview an "informant group" composed of one hundred undergraduate students at the same university, all of whom were identified in advance to be regular users of emoji, and who willingly and even enthusiastically participated in the research project for this book. The group was selected, as well, to reflect an equal number of males and females—fifty each—in the event that gender emerged as a factor in emoji usage. All informants were between eighteen and twenty-two years of age. They provided the team with 323 of their personal text messages, tweets, and other social media materials. These were offered by every informant and their usage underwent an ethics approval process for utilization in this book. Personal information has been removed from the texts and materials if it entails some compromising situation. Overall, the informant group constituted a "field laboratory" within which emoji usage could be examined directly.

Emoji writing is a product of the Internet Age, although there are precedents for analogous writing styles in previous eras, as can be seen in the illuminated texts of the Medieval and Renaissance eras (to be discussed subsequently). My objective is to assess the *raison d'être* for the rise of emoji at this time and the social and philosophical implications it might have for the interrelation among literacy, human communication, and human consciousness.

1 EMOJI AND WRITING SYSTEMS

Writing means sharing. It's part of the human condition to want to share things.

PAOLO COELHO (B. 1947)

The Oxford Dictionary's Word of the Year (see Preface) was not the only event in 2015 that brought out the growing communicative and social significance of emoji. Musicians, artists, politicians, and advertisers, among many others, started using them in their tweets, on their Facebook pages, on websites, and in other digital venues. Even a distinguished musical artist like Sir Paul McCartney, of the Beatles, was enlisted by Skype to create ten animated emoji, called "Love Mojis," for its new app. These included characters named Flirting Banana, Excited Octopus, and Sumo Cupid. As their names suggest, they were timed to appear on Valentine's Day. The emoji gyrated and wiggled to background music composed by McCartney. The Flirting Banana emoji could even be seen peeling off its own skin in a strip-teasing style.

Skype had previously introduced custom-made animated emoji that tapped into anything that was *au courant*, from images of major movie studios to those paying symbolic homage to Indian traditions. The Skype case is not atypical. Throughout modern society, there seems to be a kind of urgency to incorporate emoji to put on display a new and "cool" style of writing and communicating. And the urgency is not limited to the millennial generation who grew up in the digital world. It extends to virtually everyone, from Paul McCartney to Hillary Clinton. Emoji of the American politician were made for iPhone and Android users, and called, appropriately "Hillmoji." There is even a "World Emoji Day" on July 17 to celebrate an ever-expanding emoji culture of sorts. As far as I know, no one has ever celebrated anything of the kind in the past—a "World Vowel Day" would have seemed trivial, banal, or sarcastic by those reared in the previous Print Age.

The spread of emoji raises several key questions about how we now communicate and, more significantly, why we do so in this new comic-book style. Before even attempting to consider this question, it is useful, if not crucial, to take a step back and look at the nature and role of writing systems in human life and how they evolved. That is the main purpose of this chapter. This historical sortie will allow me to establish the theoretical framework that will be required to discuss the emoji phenomenon semiotically. So, after a brief discussion of the origins of emoji, this chapter will look at writing systems schematically, along with the social aspects of writing and its various modalities. The discussion here is restricted to bare essentials. Finally, a description of the research method and semiotic tools used for this book will conclude the chapter.

Origins of emoji

The word *emoji* is an English adaptation of Japanese 絵文字—the *e* of *emoji* means "picture" and the *moji* stands for "letter, character." So, the definition of *emoji* is, simply, a "picture-word"—a rather accurate characterization of what an emoji is. The word itself can be used as both singular and plural in English (which will be the practice in this book), although it is now also commonly pluralized (*emojis*). The first emoji symbols, as different from emoticons, were created around 1998 by a Japanese telecommunications worker named Shigetaka Kurita, who was (purportedly) an avid reader of manga comics, adapting the visually appealing manga style to replace the more graphic emoticon style. Actually, it was in 1997, the year in which internet use started becoming more and more dominant, that many users began employing ASCII emoticons on websites and in emails—ASCII stands for "American Standard Code for Information Interchange," a standard set of digital codes representing letters and symbols, used in the transfer of text between computers. That was also the year in which Nicolas Loufrani created "portrait emoticon forms" to replace the plain ones constructed with punctuation marks. Loufrani is the son of journalist Franklin Loufrani, who was the first to trademark the smiley symbol in 1972. He did so in order to put a positive spin or tone to news reportage rather than the typical pessimistic one found in print media. Right after, the smiley was adopted as a symbol of "positivity" and "cheerfulness" around the world.

For the sake of historical accuracy, it should be mentioned that the smiley was invented by an American graphic artist called Harvey Ross Ball in 1964. He created it for an insurance company who wanted to put it on buttons for its employees in order to increase their morale. The button became a craze throughout America and, eventually, the world, thus embedding the smiley image into global consciousness. In the early 1970s, mugs, T-shirts, bumper stickers (with the phrase "Have a happy day") were produced by two Philadelphia entrepreneurs, the brothers Bernard and Murray Spain. These could be seen throughout the social landscape. Then, in 1982 a group of Carnegie Mellon researchers who were using an online bulletin board to "trade quips" about events in their building, came apparently to the realization that others may have been eavesdropping and thus taken the conversation more seriously than it was intended to be. From this, so the story goes, they developed the smiley, :), to ensure that everyone would know that the message was intended to be jocular, not serious. A decade later, emoji emerged to make emoticons more pictorially complete: ☺ instead of :).

It was Kurita's emoji forms, however, that gained widespread use starting in 2010. Since 2011, when Apple launched its Operating System Five (iOS5), which included emoji characters, Kurita's picture-word symbols surged, across the spectrum of digital communication formats and across the globe. Emoji now are included on all kinds of computer keyboards. The one below is a typical example:

Keyboard with emoji characters

With the launch of Unicode 8 in 2015, which made a large repertory of picture-words available (including smileys with more skin tones), emoji use became a veritable new writing code, indicating how people communicated via the internet and mobile devices, and permeating as well many areas of society, from advertising to political campaigning. Unicode is an international encoding standard for use with different scripts—it assigns a unique number value to each character that applies across different platforms and programs, making it possible for users of different languages to use a unitary system of fonts.

As mentioned in the Preface, the rise and rapid spread of emoji might signal an incipient paradigm shift in how people perceive writing, literacy, and communication today. Unlike the Print Age, which encouraged, and even imposed, the exclusive use of alphabetic writing in most message-making media and domains of literacy, the current Internet Age encourages different modes of writing (visual and audio) to be utilized in tandem with alphabetic (and nonalphabetic) scripts in the composition of messages. This new kind of "blended writing" system harbors a broad range of implications within it, from the possible demise of the Print Age to a modern-day manifestation of the unconscious forces at work in the evolution of human communication systems and practices. The purpose of this book, as mentioned, is to grasp these implications by examining the forms, meanings, and functions of emoji, gleaning from them any relevant implications.

Since emoji are preconstructed and largely standardized pictorial characters, they can be seen to constitute a new kind of artificial, universally usable writing code. But there is much more to the emoji phenomenon than this, as will be argued throughout this book. So, it is useful to revisit here the notion of "writing system," in order to establish a point of reference for discussing if and where emoji fit in with previous writing practices that have evolved naturally—the term "artificial" is used here to allude to a writing system that has been intentionally constructed by someone instead of one that has developed over time from historical linguistic and cultural tendencies guiding its development. Moreover, emoji appear to have rather unique characteristics vis-à-vis traditional writing systems. They have both pictographic (directly representational of objects) and logographic (word-replacement) functions. As is well known, early writing was essentially pictographic, evolving in various areas of the world later into logographic, ideographic, or alphabetic systems. The shift from pictography to alphabetic writing around 1,000

BCE was designated by Marshall McLuhan (1962) as the first true cognitive paradigm shift in human history, marking the migration of humans from tribal societies to the first civilizations, which became acutely dependent on written transactions and documents for establishing their foundations and for guaranteeing their workability as new systems of communal life.

With the appearance and spread of emoji, which have now almost completely replaced emoticons, there is the possibility of a second paradigm shift in progress, characterized by a kind of retrieval of pictographic-logographic writing amalgamated with alphabetic writing. If this trend grows, and evolves into a full-fledged, picture-phonetic hybrid language, one can argue that it is laying the foundations for a new civilization—a global one based on a common visual language or, more accurately, a hybrid (or blended) writing system. If that is so, then the way we read and write messages is not only radically different from the past, but it may also indicate a dramatic shift in human consciousness, away from its linear and literal mode of processing information toward a more holistic and imaginative mode. On the other hand, emoji writing may just be a passing fad, associated with new technologies and trends in popular culture (after all they were inspired by manga comics) that allow users to make their messages more amusing and enjoyable. Their function would then be deemed to be more decorative than substantial. And as technologies change, so too do the fads, suggesting that emoji may themselves soon be a thing of the past. These questions will be broached throughout this book, but will be treated directly in the final two chapters.

Writing systems

Theories on the origins of writing abound. The history of the debates need not concern us here. There are, however, some facts and ideas that have received wide acceptance among linguists and archeologists, which are useful to the subject matter of this book. The most prominent one is that pictographic writing precedes all other kinds phylogenetically and that its emergence coincides with what scientists call "prehistoric art." If so, then writing and art might have a common origin (Bouissac 1983, 1994, 1997). To this day, we seem intuitively inclined to perceive picture writing of any type, including emoji, as somewhat artistic. This "picture writing instinct" (Dutton 2010) seems to be part of the human DNA, so to speak, manifesting itself early in life. At about the time that children utter their first words they also start scribbling and doodling without any training, if given some drawing instrument. Some claim that this may be an evolutionary residue from the distant past that unconsciously guides language development (Vygotsky 1962). The archeological record suggests that defining attributes of the human species, such as the ability to think and plan consciously and to transmit skills and knowledge across generations, coincide with the emergence of language, which appears in vocal and nonvocal forms (such as gesture) from the outset.

Many linguists (perhaps most) see vocal language as preceding written language on the evolutionary scale, considering the latter to be simply a means of recording vocal speech. As Leonard Bloomfield (1933: 21) famously put it: "Writing is not language, but merely a way of recording language by means of visible marks." However, it is no coincidence that this view is largely a product of alphabet-using societies. If the archeological and paleontological records are correct then it cannot be fully sustained, if at all. There is strong evidence that language as a mental faculty developed before vocal speech and that it was expressed through gesture and pictography. The evidence is indirect, but still persuasive. The larynx makes vocal speech physically possible. In human infants it is high in the neck, as it is in other primates. Infants breathe, swallow, and vocalize in ways that are physiologically similar to gorillas and chimps. But, at some point around the first three to six months of life, the larynx starts to descend down into the neck. The new low position means that the respiratory and digestive tracts now cross above it. This entails a few risks: food can easily lodge in the entrance of the larynx, and humans cannot drink and breathe simultaneously without choking. But in compensation, it produces a pharyngeal chamber above the vocal folds that can modify sound, making vocal speech possible.

Now, research on the casts of human skulls has established that the lowering of the larynx became a permanent feature of human anatomical development around 100,000 years ago (Laitman 1983, 1990). This strongly suggests that there may have been language without vocal speech in pre-Homo sapiens species. The most probable modes of communication were, therefore, gesture and perhaps pictography. When vocal speech became physiologically possible, it is likely that it was used in tandem with the previous gestural signs, not replacing them completely. This is the most likely reason why we still use gesture as a mode of communication (when vocal speech is impossible), and why we gesticulate when we speak. Now, whatever the relation between writing and vocal speech, suffice it to say here that both modes are used for the encoding, storage, and transfer of information. They are not mutually exclusive. The two complement each other in many ways.

Clearly, the study of writing systems has many implications for the origins and evolution of human cultures. Writing systems fall into several broad categories. Pictographic writing consists, of course, of picture signs that are made to resemble what they stand for. Ideographic writing involves the use of pictures and symbols to represent both objects and ideas, usually by combining pictographs in some way. Syllabaries are made up of characters that stand for speech syllables, thus approaching alphabet systems, and logographies consist of symbols that do not stand for a referent directly, but for the words that do. Alphabets consist of a standard set of letters, known technically as *graphemes*, representing speech units called phonemes (such as distinctive vowel and consonant sounds). Although this is a highly reductive categorization of writing systems and their modalities, it will suffice for the present purposes. Alphabets are the most "economical" of all the systems since, like the digits in the decimal or binary numerical systems, they consist of a finite set of symbols, from twenty to around thirty-five, that can be used to write all the words of a language over and over, whereas syllabaries have from eighty to one hundred symbols, and the other systems several hundreds. In alphabets, graphic symbols, known as punctuation signs, were introduced much later to aid in the layout of the written text, both as cues for word and sentence boundaries, and to signal prosodic features such as intonation and inflection. Given the abstract symbolic complexity of alphabetic systems, it is little wonder that learning and mastering them requires time and significant schooling.

Alphabetic scripts are called *linear* because they involve laying out texts in some linear form, from left-to-right, right-to-left, up-down, or down-up; nonalphabetic systems are less dependent on directional layout, because their symbols stand for concepts, rather than sounds. This does not mean that the latter systems do not possess structure. As Naomi Baron (2010) has observed, a main characteristic of alphabetic writing is that it matches the syntax of the language it transcribes, allowing for the concatenation of singular ideas into complex interrelated ones in some rule-based arrangement (Trager 1974). On the other hand, pictographic systems are less dependent on the syntax of verbal language (Mallery 1893). They are highly versatile in their ability to represent the sequential stages of episodes and actions, such as narrative ones (Diringer 1962: 21).

Research shows that a balance between visual and phonetic writing modalities emerges in most writing practices and styles (Schele 1979). The Maya, for instance, had a set of phonetically based writing symbols, which they used alongside pictographic characters. The latter were used for dynastic records, because they were easier for most people to decipher. In other words, the Maya system was a hybrid or "mixed-modal" one, whereby one script or the other was used as required to ensure that understanding would occur. The best-known ancient mixed-modal system was the Egyptian hieroglyphic one. From about 2,700 to 2,500 BCE the Egyptian hieroglyphs were mainly iconic, referring to concrete referents (eye, giraffe, sandal, reed, bread, flute, etc.). But as the system came to be used regularly, it developed numerous ideographs for referring to abstract referents (beat, cry, walk, break, bind). There was also a connection between parts of speech and actual writing forms. Concrete nouns were typically portrayed as pictographs, whereas verbs were represented by ideographs (Goldwasser 1995). Some modern scripts are more precisely "bimodal," rather than mixed modal, involving two main types of writing scripts. Japanese, for example, is written with two complete syllabaries—the hiragana and the katakana—devised to supplement the characters originally taken over from Chinese. All this suggests that writing is not an arbitrary way for representing vocal speech, but rather a highly adaptive and culturally sensitive tool for encoding information.

The first known alphabet system was the *abjad*, wherein a single symbol stood for a particular consonant. Various Semitic scripts were originally such systems. When the Phoenician abjad reached Greece, vowel symbols were added, transforming it into a more complete alphabetic script. For the sake of historical accuracy, it should be pointed out that there were also scripts called *abugidas* in other parts of the world, which also had phonetic symbols, again for consonants. There are also scripts, called *featural*, which have symbols that stand for phonetic features in sounds, such as, for example, "labiality" or "voicing." The best-known featural script is Korean *hangul*, wherein symbols are combined with alphabet characters into syllabic blocks to write words.

Alphabetic writing became the norm in Western writing practices, after the Romans adopted the Greek script and stylized it for their own purposes (Coulmas 1989). Alphabetic writing likely emerged in the marketplaces of the ancient world because it made the writing of transactions rapid and efficient. The transition was evolutionary, however, not revolutionary. Every alphabet character is the symbolic residue of a stylistic alteration to some earlier pictograph. The alphabet character, A, for instance, started out as a pictograph of the head of an ox in Egypt. This came, at some point, to be drawn only in its bare outline, and eventually standing for the word for ox (*aleph*). Around 1,000 BCE Phoenician scribes, who wrote from right-to-left, drew the ox outline sideways. The slanted Phoenician figure came to stand just for the first sound in the word (*a* for *aleph*), because it became very familiar. The Greeks, who wrote from left-to-right, turned the Phoenician figure around the other way. About 500 BCE, the A assumed the upright position it has today in Roman script.

When the Greeks started the practice of naming each symbol by such words as *alpha, beta, gamma*, which were imitations of Phoenician words (*aleph* "ox," *beth* "house," *gimel* "camel"), the concept of "alphabet" had finally crystallized in human consciousness. Because phonetic writing is laid out in a line, the direction in which the characters are written became a relevant social writing practice. The early alphabets could be written in two main directions, horizontally (left-to-right or right-to-left) or vertically (up-down). Texts were also commonly written boustrophedonically— starting in one direction and then reversing direction at the end of the line. The Greek system, and most subsequent Western alphabet writing systems, settled on the left-to-right directionality. Arabic and Hebrew texts, on the other hand, assumed a right-to-left directionality. Scripts that incorporate Chinese characters have typically been written vertically (top-to-bottom), from the right to the left of the page, but nowadays they are written in various directions, due to Western influence, a growing need to accommodate words in Latin script, and the presence of technical limitations in electronic document formats.

Alphabetic scripts have gradually incorporated various other symbols. Punctuation marks have been included to indicate nonsegmental features of speech (intonation, pause, etc.). Numerals and other nonalphabetic symbols are also used in expanded alphabetic systems. These include the percent sign (%), currency signs ($, €), and various other common signs such as the ampersand (&) and the "at" sign (@).

Writing as social practice

Needless to say, other categories and theoretical frameworks have been developed to classify and describe writing. The term *writing*, moreover, is not restricted to scripts and their features; it is also used to refer to the social practices and values connected with written representations and communications. From the outset of civilization, writing has been considered to have great social value, and thus used across time and cultural spaces to record important ideas, such as those found in sacred texts and scientific and philosophical treatises. It has always been perceived to be a semiotic medium through which authoritative or significant messages are expressed. Of course, the opposite profane and vulgar uses of writing have always existed, alongside the authoritative and sacred ones, as can be seen in the ancient graffiti messages found on ancient walls, pillars, and various artifacts. It is noteworthy at this point to observe that emoji writing is considered by many social pundits to fall into the latter category. But this does not turn out to be true, as we shall see. Emoji writing is hardly profane or vulgar; its intent is, actually, to add what can be called "visual tone" to a message. As the informants of the research group pointed out to us, emoji writing is never used, and would not be considered appropriate if it was, in formal texts, such as in school essays, official letters, or even most emails; nor would it be appropriate to use it to express vulgarities even in informal texts, although some admitted that they did use emoji in obscene ways occasionally. Thus, emoji writing is neither sacred nor profane; it is an annotative code, used largely in informal communications, to add visual annotations to the conceptual content of a message.

In the Internet Age, the popularity of mobile devices encourages writing rather than speaking for reasons that will be discussed subsequently. This means that writing has assumed many of the functions of face-to-face (F2F) communication. There are two temporalities involved in digital writing: synchronous and asynchronous. Asynchronous digital communication occurs when the receiver is not necessarily aware that a message has been sent to him or her—this characterizes emails, bulletin boards, blogs, and chat rooms. The receiver will access the message in a time-delayed fashion and then respond to it. Synchronous digital communication occurs, instead, when the receiver is aware of the communication as an ongoing one—in real rather than delayed time. F2F conversations are synchronous, influencing verbal interaction. This, however, is changing in synchronous digital communications, as the data collected on emoji writing for this book strongly suggests. Offline asynchronous communication occurs mainly in written print media (letters, books, and so on), which carry their own set of dislocated (delayed) reading patterns depending on the genre of writing. In digital communications, moreover, the receivership may involve many interlocutors, as happens when an email is sent to many people at once, or it may be aimed directly at someone exclusively.

Synchronous forms of digital communications require rapid writing, so that the back-and-forth repartee can be maintained in real time without losing the receiver's attention. This is creating new types of literacy and communicative practices based on time-saving devices such as abbreviated forms. Some observers are decrying this as a product of modern-day inertia and laziness-inducing technologies. Helprin (2009), for instance, cautions that such styles of communication produce an addictive effect on how people process information, rendering them much less pensive and reflective. Others respond that they reflect nothing more than an efficient way to create written messages for informal communication. In this view, people use abbreviated language and emoji, not to generate thoughtfulness and literary contemplation, but to make sure that written synchronous communication can occur rapidly and efficiently. In no way does this new form of writing imply that people have lost the desire to read and reflect upon the world.

To use Olson's (1977) terminology, there is a difference between "utterance meaning," which is comprehensible only in the context where the utterance occurs, and "text meaning," which entails dislocation from the context and greater control of language and content. Today's text messages, tweets, and the like have mainly an utterance function. The more textual functions of writing are still realized through traditional writing styles. Emoji serve (mainly) the utterance function, bolstering the rapidity of reading by providing visual imagery to the writing. In some ways, they have made digital interactions preferable to F2F ones. To corroborate this, we asked the informants in the research group why they often preferred to use text messages over oral conversations among friends. The following three answers—taken from all the statements made—typified the ideas expressed:

1   "It's like talking, but better, because I can edit the message before sending it."

2   "I can go back to my message to see what I wrote so that I can make sense of my friend's own message."

3   "I prefer it to speaking, which can be dangerous because I can't take back my words; this way I can, and with emoji I always try to make sure my friends understand."

Stylization

Writing systems evolve typically by expanding their modalities or styles (ways of writing). The modality of early systems is, as discussed, essentially iconic—that is, the forms are created to stand for something via resemblance, such as a drawing of the sun to stand for the actual sun. However, to make their coverage more expansive, these systems also included, or developed, elements of indexicality, such as visual forms pointing to or indicating something, and symbol signs that were used for specific ritualistic or other social needs. The first in-depth description of these three fundamental modalities in the construction of signs and sign systems comes (as is well known) from the writings of Charles S. Peirce (1931–58). It is pertinent to note that, before Peirce's semiotic usage of the term, *icon* was used in religious art to refer to the image of a sacred figure. The word still has that meaning today. Religious icons represent sacred figures not in terms of any direct resemblance to them, but rather in a generic way, without the details that would give each figure a distinctive human personality. The faces are stylized to convey somberness and piety. The same kind of stylization principle applies to even the earliest pictographs. They were not true reproductions of their referents; they were mainly outlines or sketches of them, as can be seen in the carvings of animals which cover the roofs and walls of caves, such as those at Lascaux in France and Altamira in Spain. These go back some 30,000 years. These may well be the precursors of early writing. The work of Schmandt-Besserat (1992) has shown, in fact, that the first pictographic systems were probably made possible from the creation of clay tokens, such as those discovered in Western Asia from the Neolithic era. These seem to be image-reproducing objects, much like molds or type-setting stamps, thus likely having the same functions of "character keys" today.

The topic of stylization is especially relevant to any discussion or analysis of emoji, which are essentially stylized iconic forms similar to sketches. But, their basic iconicity is expanded to include other modalities as the situation might require. For example, a *cloud* emoji is a pictographic form that suggests the outline of a cloud. A *sunrise* emoji, on the other hand, is an ideographic form, showing the shape of a sun as it rises up from a background:

Cloud emoji

Sunrise emoji

Other stylistic modalities of the emoji code include value, color, and perspective. Value refers to the darkness or lightness of a line or shape. It plays an important role in portraying contrasts of various kinds. Color conveys various modalities of meaning. In the *cloud* emoji above, the grayish-white color stands for the actual color of clouds (as we perceive it); in some emoji, however, it can suggest various emotions (such as a red face standing for anger). Perspective, as used here, refers to a simulative representation, intended to evoke some feature of perception, such as movement. The *sunrise* emoji above is designed to impart a sense of the sun moving upward.

Although emoji surfaced as a means to enhance broader comprehension of written texts in the global village, culturally stylized forms have nonetheless emerged for various reasons (as will be discussed subsequently). Take, for example, facial emoji (or smileys). By and large, the creators of smileys have attempted to make them as culturally neutral as possible. The use of yellow to color the smiley is an obvious stylistic ploy to remove recognizable facial features associated with race or ethnicity. Roundness also helps attenuate specific details of facial structure that would otherwise suggest personality or identity. But, almost right after their introduction into common usage, new emoji were constructed that embedded culturally based meanings, either explicitly or unwittingly. The *nerd* and *sleuth* emoji below, for example, require understanding what a "nerd" or "sleuth" implies in culture-specific ways. These would make absolutely no sense to, say, a tribal society living outside the realm of modern urbanized cultures from which these signs emerged. It is perhaps more accurate to say that some emoji are higher on a "universality scale" than others. The *slightly frowning* and *smiling faces* below can be located higher up on the scale, as can, perhaps, the *white frowning face*, the *face with rolling eyes*; others, such as the *robot face*, are likely to have "mid-scale" comprehensibility; and others still, such as the *Live long and prosper* emoji, are likely to have a lower-scale comprehensibility. The last emoji alludes to a pop-culture referent—the 1960s *Star Trek* program on American network television where it surfaced as the Vulcan peace sign. Although the sign has become somewhat of a common symbol in many parts of the world, its interpretation is constrained by various variables, such as the age of the emoji user and his or her geo-historical background:

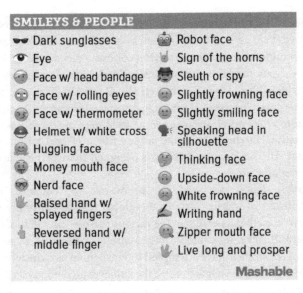

SMILEYS & PEOPLE

- Dark sunglasses
- Eye
- Face w/ head bandage
- Face w/ rolling eyes
- Face w/ thermometer
- Helmet w/ white cross
- Hugging face
- Money mouth face
- Nerd face
- Raised hand w/ splayed fingers
- Reversed hand w/ middle finger
- Robot face
- Sign of the horns
- Sleuth or spy
- Slightly frowning face
- Slightly smiling face
- Speaking head in silhouette
- Thinking face
- Upside-down face
- White frowning face
- Writing hand
- Zipper mouth face
- Live long and prosper

Mashable

Facial emoji

The *smiley* and *face with tears* emoji, used to indicate "laughing so hard I am crying," are the two facial emoji that are likely to be understood in the same way across the global village—as evidenced by the Oxford Dictionary's choice of the latter as its word of year and the fact that the smiley is found on all keyboards, no matter what language is involved.

Smiley emoji   Face with tears emoji

But, they are not "words," in any traditional sense of that word, despite the Dictionary's characterization of the *face with tears* emoji as a word. They are stylized, almost comic-book-like, pictures that can (and do) replace words and phrases. Their main function seems to be that of providing nuances in meaning in the tone of the message. So, they are not completely substitutive of traditional written forms; rather, they reinforce, expand, and annotate the meaning of a written communication, usually by enhancing the friendliness of the tone, or else by adding humorous tinges to it. In fact, when asked, "Why do you add emoji to your text messages?" the informants of our research group pointed out in unison: "To make them fun." In other words, emoji add utterance meaning to the written text—to use Olson's terminology above. Their function is thus neither purely substitutive nor decorative, as will be discussed (although they have emerged to replace certain discourse functions such as salutation as we shall see in the next chapter). They are meaning-enhancing devices that are amalgamated with alphabetic ones, turning modern-day informal writing into a unique kind of bimodal system.

Research method

In order to establish an evidence-based framework for gleaning the implications—or lack thereof—of emoji in contemporary human life, rather than basing it on subjective speculations, a qualitative research method was adopted, as mentioned in the Preface, based on limited representative sample messages, a number of semistructured interviews, and the in-depth contributions of a group of students for whom emoji are an essential part of daily digital interactions.

To reiterate briefly here, the data were collected at the University of Toronto. The data consisted of actual text messages—323 of them—written by 18- to 22-year-old university students, divided equally into fifty males and fifty females. A research team of four other students collected the texts and also carried out forays into the online world to gather other kinds of relevant information and materials to either corroborate or refute the "locally gathered" data. The team also conducted semistructured interviews with the informants. The various questions used are explained throughout this book.

Clearly, quantitative verification of the generic findings reported in this book will be required to see if they are broadly verifiable, enlarging the sample size to include the assessment of emoji use across the normal social variables (age, class, education, gender, and so on). This research project is simply a starting point. In a way, the method used here is a case study aiming to understand emoji use in a purposive or focused sample of willing participants so as to get an initial overview of the phenomenon at hand. The results will, of course, need further investigation, but there is no reason to believe that the chosen sample is vastly different from any other kind of sample.

Semiotics is used here as a generic tool for interpreting the data, not a technical one. As the discipline studying and documenting signs, sign behavior, sign creation, and sign functions, semiotics is an ideal tool for conducting an analysis of a specific set of signs (emoji). A *sign* is defined as any physical form that stands for something other than itself in some specific context. One of its modern-day founders, the Swiss philologist Ferdinand de Saussure, defined semiotics as the science concerned with "the role of signs as part of social life" and "the laws governing them" (Saussure 1916: 15). In this book the term *symbol* is often used in alternation with *sign,* unless a particular sign is to be specified as something other than a symbol. Technical notions, when needed, will be defined or illustrated as clearly as possible.

2 EMOJI USES

Shyness is fueled in part by so many people spending huge amounts of time alone, isolated on e-mail, chat rooms, which reduces their face-to-face contact with other people.

PHILIP ZIMBARDO (B. 1933)

In 2015, the Oxford Dictionary's choice of the *face with tears of joy* emoji was not the only event that appeared to have significance. Another rather striking event was a trial in that year of a California man charged with operating an online black-market bazaar. During the course of the trial, which took place in New York City, the lawyer of the accused raised an objection suggesting that a critical piece of evidence was omitted by the trial prosecutors—namely, a smiley. The objection arose after a prosecutor had finished reading an internet post written by the accused, making no mention of the happy-face emoji that accompanied it. The intent of the lawyer was to argue that the use of the emoji showed that his client was not being serious, but rather playful, and thus that there really was no criminal intent in the first place. The judge instructed the jury that it should take into account any such symbols in messages. In a phrase, an emoji was allowed in a court of law as evidence about someone's intended meaning, and thus, as revelatory about someone's state of mind as verbal statements or admissions.

This was an explicit acknowledgment that emoji were now part of how we express ourselves and thus also usable as evidence in court trials. In the same year, the Pittsburgh police also presented three emoji in a text message as evidence in a double-homicide trial. The prosecutors argued that the emoji would help prove that the person who sent it, who was himself shot during the commission of a robbery, was responsible for the deadly gunfire. The message-sender spent five days in a coma before regaining consciousness. The prosecutors claimed that the emoji he sent before the shooting showed that he intended to participate in the robbery that led to the killings. The emoji depicted a man running, an explosion, and a gun.

These two trials indicate, above all else, that we now take emoji use seriously, and thus that they add more than "decorative trimmings," so to say, to written messages. We now perceive them to be laden with emotional and discourse functions of all kinds, including the conveyance of intent, mood, and state of mind. They are, therefore, revelatory signs of how we think and intend to act. When the research team presented this to the informants, many of whom already knew about the trials, the reaction stated by one of the informants encapsulated what all the others also thought: "Emoji tell a lot about us today, don't they?"

This chapter will look at a few basic discourse functions of emoji. A more detailed analysis of such functions will be elaborated in subsequent chapters. The goal here is simply to show how general emoji use is now part of utterance meaning, indicating how it may have taken over the specific functions of verbal formulas, such as those used in salutation and the expression of some emotions. The chapter also discusses the appearance of ambiguity in the emoji code and how attempts to resolve this have been carried out. Ambiguity in the code has rather profound implications for its purported universality, given that one of the goals of artificial languages is to diminish, or potentially eliminate, ambiguity in verbal interactions.

Phatic function

Discourse is the use of language for social and psycho-emotional reasons. It typically reveals much more than the sum of the parts of which it is made. It belies belief systems, ideologies, worldviews, and above all else, provides insights into how people extract meaning from interactions. By studying the discourse functions and uses of emoji in specific text messages, we can surmise what they add to common digital exchanges and what this implies.

From even a cursory analysis of the 323 texts provided by the informants, it became obvious that emoji use in strategic locations in a text message allows for critical discourse functions to take place in a visually effective way, as we shall see throughout this book. The one that stands out, and which requires attention from the outset, is the enactment of the *phatic* function of discourse (Jakobson 1960). In other words, emoji usage seems to constitute, above all else, a visually based version of "small talk" that is used typically for establishing social contact and for keeping the lines of communication open and pleasant. This aspect of common discourse was first studied by the anthropologist Bronislaw Malinowski (1923), who coined the term "phatic communion" to characterize such talk as a social skill. Phatic speech is a crucial aspect of bonding rituals and a means for putting forth what the sociologist Erving Goffman (1955) termed a "positive social face" during communicative interaction. So, for example, a smiley used at the beginning of a text message provides a basis on which to present such a face and to imbue the tone of the message with positivity, thus ensuring that bonding between the interlocutors is maintained. It lubricates the ensuing communicative exchange, so to speak, by keeping it friendly.

A more detailed analysis of the student texts showed that the following three phatic functions of emoji are the most common ones:

1 *Utterance opener.* The smiley (or a similar emoji) is used in place of opening salutations such as "Hi!" allowing the sender to present (literally) a positive face and thus to imbue the message with a cheerful tone or mood. Such emoji are designed to strengthen or maintain friendly bonds between interlocutors even when (and perhaps more so) a message may have some negativity in its contents.

2 *Utterance ending.* A quick message, such as a typical text message or tweet, generally ends abruptly, and thus there is a risk that the sender may be appearing to reject or rebuff the receiver. So, the smiley (again) is used typically as the "good-bye" function in a message, thus allowing the sender to mitigate the danger of conveying any implicit sense of rejection, affirming the friendly bond that exists between the interlocutors.

3 *Silence avoidance.* In face-to-face conversations, many people tend to interpret moments of silence as uncomfortable or awkward. So, a typical discourse solution is to fill these "silence gaps" with meaningless expressions ("The weather is really changing, isn't it?" "Time is really flying these days," and so on). In written messages, the equivalent of silence gaps occurs when the receiver expects more information about something, whereas

the sender wishes to avoid it. By putting emoji in such content gaps, the intent is to counteract the uncomfortableness that may result from them.

As these basic phatic functions of emoji indicate, their main use is to keep interactions friendly and cheerful. They are thus used mainly in informal written texts exchanged among social peers such as friends, colleagues, and family members. They are not used in formal texts such as essays, treatises, scientific papers, and so on. If they were to be used in them, their usage would likely be interpreted as ironic or even cynical.

Emoji use is also peer- and age-sensitive. When I asked the informants what they would think if I were to use them in my text communications with them, I received two general answers that are encapsulated by the comments of one particular informant as follows: (1) "It would seem a bit weird;" (2) "It might show that you are trying to be friendly, but it's still weird." And when I asked why this was so, the answer was: (3) "You're a bit old." So, I then asked with whom they would use emoji regularly. The chart below summarizes their answers:

Communication function	Number of informants
Communication with friends	100
Communication with family	89
Other	12

In the "Other" category the main usage was on dating sites—a function indicated by only a few of the older members of the group (six of the twelve indicated "Other"). So, for example, if a question such as, "Want to meet up"?, was put forward by one of the interlocutors wanting to date the other, the three emoji below might be used to accompany such a question (as three of the informants indicated):

Romance emoji

Clearly, each one conveys a different romantic mood or intent. The one to the left, with its "heart eyes," communicates a simple sense of romantic love, usually associated with the "infatuated face;" the middle one adds a touch of salaciousness to this basic face, via the tongue hanging out of the mouth, suggesting a sense of lustfulness or covetousness; and the one to the right constitutes a "flirtatious winking" face, along with a wry sense of playful romantic involvement through its knowing, impish smile. These emoji bring out a theme that will be discussed subsequently, namely that they add clever semantic nuances to a written message. Above all else, they impart a cheery tone to a romantic message, thus alleviating the risk of conveying vulgarity or lewdness. Even the middle one transmits suggestive lustfulness in an amusing and thus perceptively harmless way. So, these emoji have the same basic phatic function of imbuing messages with jollity, thus attenuating any potential conflictual content.

The phatic function of emoji stands out as a systematic one—virtually all the text messages analyzed started out with a smiley and ended in a similar way. They seem to have replaced the traditional salutation markers. In fact, we did not find one text message that started off only with a written salutation protocol such as "Hi;" and when it did, an emoji accompanied it.

Emotive function

The romantic emoji above in particular reveal that the "control of emotions," so to speak, is a primary discourse function of some, if not most, emoji. They also suggest that conveying one's state of mind (opinion, judgment, attitude, outlook, sentiments, etc.) is a basic need in discourse exchanges. To use another of Jakobson's (1960) terms, emoji usage entails *emotivity* (consciously or unconsciously) in addition to the phatic function. This is defined as the use of discourse structures (words, intonations, phrasings, etc.) to portray one's state of mind. In face-to-face communication, people use interjections, intonation, and other prosodic strategies, alongside specific keywords and phrases, to convey their feelings, explicitly or implicitly. In informal digital messages, these are often replaced by emoji forms. The following text message provided by an informant is a case in point:

Text message-1

The insertion of four emoji signs standing for different alcoholic beverages after the phrase "I drink!!!!" does not have pure illustrative value; rather, it reveals the sender's state of mind and perspective on drinking. This amalgamation of alphabetic punctuation (the repeated exclamation points) with the emoji images constitutes an emotive speech act, suggesting the writer's probable dread and reprehension of such beverages. The *coffee* emoji combined with the *angry-disappointed face* emoji is a self-contained phrase, relaying the kind of drink (coffee) that is the correct one and the disappointment felt by the sender that this is not the case at hand ("Oops" = "I should have had coffee instead").

An overall analysis of the 323 texts provided by the informants, classified according to discourse function, reveals that the primary utilizations of emoji are to convey emotivity and to maintain phatic cohesion. The statistics were compiled by simply classifying the function of a specific emoji in a text as either phatic, emotive, or other:

1 Emoji with phatic function: 88%

2 Emoji with emotive function: 94%

3 Emoji with some other function: 64%

The emotivity of emoji can be broken down further into two subcategories: (1) as substitutes for facial expressions in F2F communications or their corresponding graphic punctuation marks in written communications; (2) to visually emphasize a point of view. While emotive emoji may seem to be totally additive or annotative to the main written message, and thus easily removable from it, the research project made it obvious that they convey much more emotional force than would otherwise be possible, while keeping the tone friendly. The above drink emoji involve criticism, but the fact that the criticism unfolds in a visual way makes us skirt around the more negative emotions that words would elicit. As mentioned, emoji allow interlocutors to control the emotional features of discourse. We asked the informant who wrote the message why she used the emoji rather than words; her answer was rather perceptive: "The emoji allowed me to criticize without anger and thus not upsetting my friend!" It is relevant to note, that our findings were corroborated by research conducted by the keyboard app Swiftkey in 2015. Swiftkey found, in fact, that 70 percent of emoji use was to express positive emotion (15 percent neutral and only 15 percent negative).

Given the importance of the emotive function, it is useful to provide a list of the most common or recurring facial emoji found in the text-message data for the purpose of simple illustration and as a framework for future discussions in this book. These are also found commonly on websites and the keyboards (or apps) of mobile devices.

Emoji	Meaning/Function
	Smiling-Happy Faces: These are often used together to convey high levels of happiness.
	Smiling Face With Open Mouth And Cold Sweat: This also conveys a sense of happiness, but with a nuance of relief. It is often found in texts that portray some negative event that, however, has turned out positively.
	Face With Tears Of Joy: This is, as mentioned several times, Oxford Dictionary's 2015 Word of the Year; it is used to convey laughter, seemingly replacing the text-message abbreviation "lol" (laugh out loud). It is used commonly in response to a joke or a funny situation.
	Smirking Face: This is used in romantic-sexual messages, providing flirtatious innuendo or entendre to the content.
	Winking Face: This suggests that a word, line, or entire message should not be taken seriously; it has a humorous or flirtatious intent.

Emoji	Meaning/Function
	Smiling Face With Sunglasses: This is used to convey "coolness" or a sense of composure or aplomb.
	Flushed Face: This conveys embarrassment or awkwardness; it might also be used to show humility in response to a compliment.
	Devil Faces: Although these are used interchangeably, the smiling one adds the nuance of naughtiness, whereas the frowning one adds a connotation of mischievousness. The purple color, rather than the generic and bland yellow one, is intended to add infernal and devilish connotations to the meaning.
	Smiling Face With Heart-Shaped Eyes: This is used typically to convey affection, love, or gratitude.
	Face With Cold Sweat: This conveys stress; in the data it was found typically in messages that indicate that some essay is overdue or that a test is coming up.
	Neutral Faces: These are used to show indifference or the state of being unimpressed by something.
	Unamused Face: This conveys suspicion, disappointment, or displeasure. It was found consistently in reaction to excuses given by an interlocutor.
	Crying Face: This constitutes a "hurt" reaction to some message.
	Loudly Crying Face: This imparts a more intense feeling of being hurt than the one above. It is often used with ironic or satirical intent.
	Worried Face: This communicates not only worry, but also shock and fear.
	Angry and Pouting Faces: These are used often together to convey anger, with the red one being the stronger one.
	Frowning Face and Anguished Face: These are used interchangeably to express shock or disappointment.

Emoji allow for emotivity to be inserted in a systematic fashion in the contents of a message, much like prosodic markers in vocal language. The question becomes whether or not such emoji are going to spread across linguistic registers, in addition to the informal ones. According to most of the informants (ninety-two of them), these will not spread because, as one of them put it, "Writings such as essays are too serious for emojis to be used." This may, in fact, be empirically correct since a perusal of formal texts online, from educational blogs to digital platform sites for scholarly and scientific papers, showed no evidence whatsoever of emoji use. So, it seems fairly safe to say that such use is constrained to the informal register (at least for now). The discourse functions of emoji will be taken up again in Chapter 6.

It is interesting to note that emoji use is not restricted to texts written in alphabetic script. They were found as well in those written by some of the bilingual students in the sample with different kinds of scripts, such as the Chinese or Korean ones. In this book, the analysis and discussion will be limited to English alphabetic writing, simply for the sake of convenience. The research team also found the use of emoji throughout scripts and languages in an online search of social media sites. Interestingly, the emoji providers are now creating forms that are specific to different languages and their cultures. This is an obvious response to the growth and spread of the emoji code across the global village. Thus, while the original intent of the emoji code may have been that of facilitating global communications, irrespective of language, it is being shaped more and more along the lines of natural languages. Some forms are universal, as we shall see, but others are language specific. So, it is more accurate to say that, today, there is a standardized emoji lexicon that is accompanied by various regionalized variants for culture-specific usage (as will be discussed below).

Standardization

The widespread use of emoji became practicable in 2010 when hundreds of emoji characters were standardized in the Unicode Standard version 6.0 and in the related ISO/IEC 10646, both of which specify the universal character set for the world's languages. The emoji additions were requested by Google and Apple to ensure that they could be used across all, or most, languages. The objectives and mission of Unicode are stated explicitly on its website.

> The Unicode Consortium is a non-profit corporation devoted to developing, maintaining, and promoting software internationalization standards and data, particularly the Unicode Standard, which specifies the representation of text in all modern software products and standards. The Unicode Consortium actively develops standards in the area of internationalization including defining the behavior and relationships between Unicode characters. The Consortium works closely with W3C and ISO—in particular with ISO/IEC/JTC 1/ SC2/WG2, which is responsible for maintaining ISO/IEC 10646, the International Standard synchronized with the Unicode Standard.

As we saw with the 323 texts, the basic emoji lexicon is in fact uniform (or "unicoded") in the sense that the forms are alike across keyboards and apps (with minor variations in detail) and thus that everyone will be impelled to use them in similar discursive ways (as we also saw above). Additional characters are created almost on a daily basis, and these are accessed primarily on online dictionaries and inventories that allow for selection and, in some cases, even modification of emoji for personalized or specialized use.

It is the standardized lexicon that has allowed the emoji code to migrate beyond Japan. But its popularity and spread has caused pressure to add culture-sensitive designs into the Unicode Standard to meet the demands of different nations and their languages. This has obvious implications for the status of the emoji code as a universal visual language (as will be discussed subsequently). Once culturally based interpretations of even the standard lexicon forms are taken into account, the purported universality of the code decreases even more so. Recalling the discussion from the previous chapter, it is more accurate to say that emoji forms fall on a universality scale, from high to low. The facial emoji above would seem to fall on the higher echelons of the scale, whereas many of the others likely fall on the lower points in the scale. Some of the forms, actually, are grafts from preexisting Webding and Wingding fonts on computers, which presumably were inserted to allow for usage by everyone as part of pre-Unicode messenger systems used not only in Japan, but across the world.

There is a constant ongoing amplification of the emoji lexicon to include variation of all kinds. Recently, Unicode 8.0 added emoji of sports equipment such as the cricket bat, food items such as the taco, signs of the Zodiac, new facial expressions, and symbols for places of worship—all of which take the code farther down, overall, on the universal scale. Nonetheless, it seems that the diversity of interpretations in emoji, when compared with the diversity found typically in the corresponding words, is somewhat attenuated. We asked the informant group to comment on Unicode 8.0's addition of new characters and of the technical ability of individual users to change, say, the skin tone of smileys and the expression of faces in general. The three answers below were typical of the overall responses;

1 "No big deal. I actually didn't know that cricket was an important sport in some parts of the world. I would never use that emoji, because I don't need it. If I did, I would, though."

2 "The skin tones are neat. I'm black and I appreciate it, but I still mainly use the yellow smileys; they seem more usable. I will use the black skin ones only when I want to convey my sense of pride in my racial identity, especially if the occasion comes up."

3 "Wasted! Aren't emojis all about simple things? Why complicate them with all these politically correct uses? I'm saying this even though I am Indian in origin."

Thus, while cultural diversity has become inherent in the expanding emoji code, there seems to be disinterest in the politics behind it by users, who genuinely seem to want to communicate as unambiguously and effectively (emotively) as possible. As one other informant put it, "Emoji work best when you don't have to think about these things." In other words, the new culturally sensitive signs are seen as options in highly contextualized messages; they are not seen as impugning the universality of the overall code. They form an optional subdomain of the code, rather than an amplification. Another problem, albeit somewhat minor, is that emoji characters vary slightly among platforms, albeit within the limits imposed by the Unicode specification system, as people and groups attempt to provide creative and artistic presentations of ideas and objects through diverse emoji forms. One of these, as we shall see, is in the advertising domain, which has adopted and adapted the emoji code for its specific purposes.

So, in sum, it is correct to say that there is now a standard emoji lexicon with many variant additions to it, which can be adopted for specific uses among certain types of interlocutors and for diverse social functions (such as in advertising). There are now several online venues that provide standard or quasi-standard emoji repertoires. One of the members of the research team found the list below on an online venue that, apparently, is a very popular one. It actually shows, ironically, how much cultural and even dated information is unavoidable in any code. Emoji referring, for example, to an alien, an old computer disk (an anachronism), a teddy bear, a rubber duck, and others, bear meaning in specific historical and cultural ways. This kind of variation may be inevitable as the emoji code becomes more and more globalized.

An online emoji lexicon

Diversification of the emoji lexicon is being brought about primarily by marketplace and political pressures, as people and brands use emoji more and more to tap into new markets, audiences, interest groups, and the like. Those who have grown up in a world where mobile devices, the internet, and social media have always existed are likely to be the main users of emoji, although, as we shall see, their spread is not only a matter of age, but of necessity and, above all else, trendiness.

Ambiguity

One of the primary dangers to the universality of the emoji code, in addition to culture-specific variation, is the constant potential for ambiguity. Ambiguous messages are dangerous, potentially, even among those who share the same language; but the danger increases in the intercultural context of the global village.

The exchange of verbal messages (spoken or written) between individuals from different linguistic and cultural backgrounds by means of a common language, such as English, are often problematic or awkward because of the tendency of the individuals participating in them to use the words and structures of the common language either as carriers of their own culture-specific meanings or with inappropriate random meanings due to a lack of knowledge of the whole range of possible meanings they entail within the common language. Consider, as a simple example, the English word *affair*, which can mean a series of things, such as the following (from Danesi and Rocci 2009: 9):

1 something done or to be done (as in "Get your *affairs* in order")

2 a professional or public transaction (as in "*affairs* of state")

3 a social occurrence or event (as in "Their wedding was a big *affair*")

4 a romantic or sexual relationship (as in "Theirs was a steamy *affair*")

Now, let's assume that two speakers, A and B, enter into a dialogue. A speaks a non-Indo-European language, having studied English as a subject in school, while B is a native speaker of English, and knows no other language. Having learned only meaning (1) above for *affair*, A makes the following statement during our hypothetical conversation: "I am involved in an affair right now, and thus cannot help you out." Upon hearing this statement, speaker B might interpret *affair* in terms of meaning (4), rather than (1), since the way the sentence was put together suggests this meaning to a native speaker of English. So, B assumes that A is involved in a romantic relationship and, because of this strange reason, will not be able to help him out. The reason given by A will in effect seem bizarre to B, since in normal English parlance it is unlikely that a romantic affair would be given as an excuse for opting out of something; but it is nevertheless likely to be accepted by B as A's genuine excuse because of the form in which it was uttered. Needless to say, any dialogical follow-up to A's sentence will predictably be colored by this miscommunication of meaning.

The linguist Bar-Hillel (1960) used an example of ambiguity that has come to be known as the *Bar-Hillel Paradox*, in order to bring out the ever-present danger of ambiguity in common speech acts. The paradox is that humans use extra-linguistic information to make sense of messages. In other words, context is a determinant in how we understand verbal signs and interpret their meanings. His example was as follows:

1 "The *pen* is in the box" (= the writing instrument is in the container)

2 "The box is in the *pen*" (= the container is inside another container [playpen])

Native speakers of English can distinguish between the two messages because they have access to outside information about the nature of pens, and this is worked into the meanings of the word *pen*—a feature called polysemy, which produces ambiguity that is resolved by real-world knowledge when it occurs in messages.

Culture coding

Studies on polysemy have shown that ambiguity is not always resolved even in discourse among native speakers. The goal of a universal emoji code has always been to help people avoid ambiguity, which is potentially destructive of human relations. But recent (and now famous) cases of ambiguity have been documented, primarily in media venues. For example, the idea of using yellow as the nondescript color of facial emoji is a transparent attempt to eliminate any possible ethnic-racial innuendo to messages (as mentioned). It is assumed that people of any ethnicity or race would use them for purely communicative reasons without the political-sociological baggage that coloring might add to them. This goal, as we have seen with our informants—a mix of Caucasian, African-Canadian, Indian, Pakistani, Iranian, Slavic, Chinese, Korean, and other ethnicities—was clearly understood by all of them. As one Pakistani informant pointed out: "It's good not to have to think in stereotypical ways when I use emoji."

Culture coding, however, invariably comes up. This is the interpretation of the same forms in specific cultural ways. For example, the *nail polish* emoji has been found to have a whole array of unwanted sexual connotations that users in some non-English-speaking countries want to avoid, finding the emoji offensive:

Nail polish emoji

The *thumbs-up* emoji is another problematic one.

The thumbs-up emoji

This seemingly universal gesture is hideously offensive in parts of the Middle East, West Africa, Russia, and South America. In many of these areas, it is the equivalent of using the middle finger in the Western world. The list of such culturally coded emoji is an extensive one, and need not concern us here. The point is that along with ambiguity, cultural coding is likely unavoidable in emoji-based discourse. It is part of human semiosis—the production, comprehension, and use of signs—which varies across the world. Often the same sign forms (such as the thumbs-up one) spring up in different places, but they have vastly different meanings assigned to them depending on context. To use the terminology introduced by Saussure (1916), the same *signifier* (a physical form such as the thumbs-up emoji) will have different *signifieds* (conceptual meanings), as per speech community.

Unicode manuals actually provide notes on the auxiliary culturally coded meanings of an emoji such as the ones above to guide users. For example, some users may use the "seat" emoji to stand for a ticket reservation rather than a sitting device. When we asked the informants about the *nail polish* emoji, the three answers below seem to indicate that it is a moot point, since it can be avoided in those countries where portrayals of female sexuality differ contrastively:

1   "Who cares about nail polish? I never use it. Nothing changes for me in using the other emoji."

2   "I've used it only once to tell my friends that I bought some nail polish. That's it. No other meaning for me!"

3   "I guess you can interpret it in many ways, but not when it is put after a word or sentence that provides the context."

3 EMOJI COMPETENCE

Brevity is the soul of wit.

WILLIAM SHAKESPEARE (1564–1616)

Since 2010, emoji have become a staple of digital communications everywhere. According to a 2015 study by the British app developer, SwiftKey, which collected and examined over a billion bits of data from Android and iOS devices in sixteen languages, 45 percent of all messages contained happy-face emoji, such as smileys, followed by sad faces, hearts, hand gestures, and romantic emoji. This finding empirically corroborates the discussion in the previous chapter that the basic use of emoji is to add a largely emotional tone to text messages, or else to add connotative nuances to the specific parts of their content. The statistical blog "FiveThirtyEight" provided even more supporting empirical data in the same year, finding that the *hearts* emoji was used in nearly 350 million tweets followed by the *joy* emoji (nearly 280 million), and the *unamused* emoji (nearly 140 million).

Given the obvious popularity and broad usage of emoji, the images are spreading to all domains of social interaction and symbolism. Big manufacturers are adopting and adapting the emoji code as part of enhancing their brand image. The International House of Pancakes, for instance, recently changed its logo to an emoji-stylized one. As can be seen below, it has the form of a smiley:

International House of Pancakes Logo

Pop culture, from where they emanated originally (from manga comic-book style), has adopted emoji as a new form of "lingo." For instance, the Canadian pop singer, Carly Rae Jepsen released a video of her song "Run Away with Me" that allows viewers to click on emoji to guide them along the scenes—that is, it allows them to determine what she does next in the video. This type of example is spreading throughout the cultural landscape. Emoji have become so much a part of that landscape that they are even provoking sociopolitical reactions of all kinds.

An example of the latter from 2016 is when *Always* (a female brand for hygienic products) launched its "Like a Girl" ad campaign designed to impart confidence in pubescent girls. The brand strategically released a video series in which teenage girls discuss the inherent gender bias in society, manifesting itself, for example, in how the emoji code reveals this very bias by depicting females typically as wearing pink clothing or getting haircuts. In one of the videos, a young woman remarks, "There's no girls in the professional emojis, unless you count being a bride a profession." Another one decries that "Girls love emojis, but there aren't enough emojis to say what girls do." Overall, the adolescent females on the video can be witnessed protesting that new emoji are needed depicting women in professions and various walks of life. This sentiment was echoed by First Lady Michelle Obama who, after seeing the videos, called for "a girl studying emoji."

Obviously, the emoji code is evolving into something different than its original intent to provide a simple picture-word system of universally comprehensible symbols for facilitating global communications. As it has turned out, the emoji code is taking on all kinds of uses and functions, leading more and more to its diversification in response to social pressures and trends that are reshaping it along the lines of natural languages. Proposals for new emoji currently have to be approved and designed by the Unicode Consortium. They are then added to the ever-expanding lists that are then added to apps and other social media tools. This implies a standardized and centralized tracking system that is, however, open to innovation and expansion. However, the code is expanding even beyond this system, as new emoji are being created regularly from all quarters of society, making their way to various websites where they can be copied and used for all kinds of digital communications.

Variation in codes is inevitable. Before dealing in more detail with this inevitability in subsequent chapters, it is useful to step back and look at the general features of the emoji code itself and how it has evolved in only a few years. Knowledge of how to use this code is now an unconsciously crystallizing system with its rules, much like those of natural languages. A code is a system of signs or sign forms and specific rules for using them. The alphabet code, for example, entails knowledge of a specific kind in order to be used meaningfully. For instance, if one were to ask a Roman alphabet user, What comes after G?, he or she would immediately be able to answer H. The user knows this because he or she is familiar with the sign forms (letters) of the alphabet and because over time he or she has become familiar with the order in which they are organized within the code. Moreover, the user knows how to select a letter in combination with other letters to write words and understand the underlying principle of alphabets (namely that each letter stands, more or less, for a phoneme). The alphabet is a perfect example of a code—a system of signs that are perceptibly distinct and that can be combined in specific ways to make words.

Use of any code, like the alphabet one, clearly requires a specific kind of knowledge, which linguists call "linguistic competence." Analogously, it is becoming increasingly obvious that there is now an "emoji competence," which entails knowledge of how to use the images to make messages with them or to locate them in written messages that both make sense and are easily interpretable by receivers. So, this chapter will look at the basic features of emoji competence, including how the emoji code is evolving in its forms and uses to expand its utterance functions.

General features

What does it mean to be "competent" in emoji? As discussed schematically in previous chapters, it implies in part knowledge of how to intersperse emoji images into a written text in order to imprint a positive emotional tone into it or to maintain phatic communion with interlocutors. The research studies mentioned above confirm that this is indeed the primary aspect of emoji competence, given its apparent universality in cross-linguistic usage. Indeed, the displacement of a smiley in a text would be seen as anomalous or nonsensical, as would a sentence constructed with words out of place or with no semantic connection to each other. The rules of emoji usage have emerged, like those of a natural language, through the usage itself. Undoubtedly, should the code continue to be used broadly, then its systematicity would be institutionalized in emoji grammars and elaborated through emoji theories. For the present, the rules of emoji usage are implicit ones emerging from uses and, largely, by the fact that they follow many of the rules of natural language syntax and semantics, as will be discussed subsequently.

Actually, emoji competence is more than concrete knowledge of how to select and combine emoji forms in specific ways; it also involves a form of what linguists call "communicative competence," or knowledge of how the forms enact communicative functions. This constitutes tacit knowledge of how to use the code effectively. Actually, today most linguists would see these two competencies—linguistic and communicative—as interactive rather than as mutually exclusive ones.

Competence in the use of any code implies, first and foremost, the ability to select and combine its forms and structures in specific ways to construct messages in meaningful ways. The emoji code is a kind of visual alphabet code providing characters that can be used in two main ways to create meaningful structures: (1) adjunctively within a written text; or (2) substitutively of such a text. Adjunctive texts, such as the texts provided by the informants, are constructed with a blend of written (alphabetic) forms and emoji ones located at specific points in the flow of the message. The kind of competence required to decode such a text is likely to be more accessible to anyone—emoji users or not. The smiley found at the end of an adjunctive text can easily be interpreted to be a salutation with positive communicative overtones. On the other hand, a substitutive text requires much more familiarity with the meanings and uses of the emoji code. The text below is a typical example, provided by the website: http://www.freemake.com:

Substitutive emoji text

As this kind of text immediately brings out, it takes a firm control of the emoji code in order to comprehend it or even just "read it" verbally. For those who are not regular users of emoji, it would take a radical retraining of their "alphabet-conditioned eyes" to understand this message. In other words, without knowledge of the code, it is virtually impossible to decipher the message, even though it follows a narrative flow that could be told with words instead. This is why one can at the very least surmise its content, more so than if it were laid out in a nonfamiliar script, which would completely preclude decipherment, bringing out that, even in substitutive writing, the emoji code has more universal features in it than has any alphabetic script. It would take very little training to impart emoji competence to virtually anyone; it takes much more to do the same when it comes to natural language competence. So, although the emoji code may be developing variation within it, as mentioned above, it still has enough universal properties built implicitly into it, given its picture-word nature, to make it much more amenable to interpretation than alphabet-based texts.

Let's start with the most easily decipherable emoji in the text. First, the writer is a speaker of English, not only because the verbal title of the passage is "Here is my emoji birth story," but also because: (a) its layout from left to right and up-down, is identical to alphabetically constructed texts in that language, and (b) many of the symbols are clearly allusive to any English-speaking culture, including the symbol for golf. The first emoji also shows that the maker of the message is a female, thus providing much more information than would the corresponding verbal pronoun "I" of English. The various facial emoji in the text can be seen to have the same functions of typical adjunctive emoji—they add emotional tone or visual annotation to the contents. Clearly, these are used in both written and emoji-constructed texts. They require no special analysis here; as already discussed they provide a range of emotional tones, from happiness to sadness, anger, and sarcasm, and are inserted in similar locations to their uses in adjunctive texts. Also, easily interpretable are concrete emoji such as the *thumbs-up* one (indicating satisfaction or approval), the fire and explosion images, which likely indicate an ardent or perhaps a volatile reaction to something, among others.

To decipher the remaining emoji, one must decode them in terms of "layout structure," paralleling sentence structure. For example, the series of images at the end consisting of a chick hatching from an egg followed by the symbol for celebration, the thumbs-up sign, the dancing symbol, and the portrait of a family constitutes a veritable syntagm—a linguistic unit consisting of a set of forms that are in a sequential relationship to one another. In all likelihood, this syntagm is interpretable as the happiness reactions and sentiments that ensue from a birth. The remaining emoji are interpreted in this way (syntagmatically). Overall, the text can be seen to relate the maker's story about how she was born and what kinds of concepts it evoked for her. Trying, though, to figure out how to translate the entire text into words clearly requires quite a bit of familiarity with similar kinds of constructed texts and the underlying code that makes them readable "to the trained eye." It requires, in other words, a high degree of emoji competence. It shows that the selection of the forms is intertwined with their distribution in the structure of the text and with how they relate to each other via meaning associations of various kinds (such as relating a chick birth with birth in general). These are the basic features that govern how we put any kind of text together—selection, combination, and associative relation. And these are certainly intrinsic to emoji competence in general.

Adjunctive texts are obviously much more amenable to broad interpretation, even on the part of nonusers of emoji, than are substitutive ones, since their use and meaning are governed more by the flow of the written message than by inherent principles of emoji structure and use. Some adjunctively created messages, however, are becoming more and more engaging cognitively, showing the use of what can be called a "mixed textuality," whereby the written text is used in tandem with emoji that do not have just adjunctive function, but are designed to substitute content in specific ways. These will be discussed in due course. For now, it is sufficient simply to provide an illustration of such a text, taken from the http://www.smosh.com/ website:

Example of a "mixed textuality" text

As can be seen, the text is laid out as any written text, but in this case the emoji are not simple add-ons, but rather substitutive structures. A decoding of the text requires rather sophisticated knowledge of the rhetorical range of signs and symbols, such as words, in a language (and its culture). The use of the *book* emoji as a "story" is the first example of this kind; the syntagm consisting of the *round-and-round* plus the *up* and *down* indexical emoji is the equivalent of a metaphorical statement such as "round and round, up and down." So, the sentence can be decoded, more or less as: "Now this is a story about how my life got turned around, up and down." The remainder of the text requires the same kind of rhetorical knowledge, such as the use of an hourglass as a metaphor for "time." As can be seen, mixed texts are more interpretable broadly than are purely substitutive ones, but they still require a high degree of emoji competence.

As this last text demonstrates, implicit in emoji use is rhetorical structure. Indeed, it can be claimed that the five traditional canons of rhetorical language can be easily discerned in emoji usage:

1 *Inventio* (invention): This is the search for an argument (topic) of a discourse or communication. It is the initial process that guides the interlocutor in forming and developing an effective argument. As we saw above, the emoji code certainly conforms to the invention canon, since it allows the sender to shape the emotive flow of the argument with rhetorical force. In the birth story text, the images and sentiments that the birth evokes are organized into a sequence of picture-words that both tell the story narratively and metaphorically. In the mixed text, the maker clearly felt that the images were much more powerful rhetorically than their corresponding verbal metaphors, given perhaps that we have become so accustomed to their usage in verbal utterances that they may have lost their rhetorical force.

2 *Dispositio* (arrangement): This is the organization of the forms of speech used in the construction of a text in order to ensure maximum persuasion. This kind of know-how is certainly evident in the emoji texts analyzed so far. The distribution of the images in the birth story text show a keen knowledge of how to emphasize the sentiments involved in the story, and the images in the mixed text show, by their specific locations, that the interlocutor wanted to emphasize certain concepts through the rhetorical senses of the emoji.

3 *Elocutio* (style): This is the process of determining how the arguments are to be presented. The friendly and sometimes comical style that emoji inject into a message directly is clearly a form of *elocutio*. The mixed text employs the emoji both to evoke a sense of humor and to provide visual annotation to the maker's state of mind.

4 *Memoria* (memory): This refers traditionally to the memorization of the text so that it can be delivered orally without notes. While this may not seem to be an operative canon in emoji text making, there is evidence that the use of emoji enhances memory of the text and guides the process of interaction. The research team asked the 100 informants if they could recall some of their recent texts, many of which were really about everyday trivial matters, and most were able to recall them almost *verbatim*, as we checked their recall against the actual texts.

5 *Actio* (delivery): This is the process of familiarizing oneself with the modes of delivery of arguments, including gesture and tone. If nothing else, the emoji code is a "tonal" picture language, since it invariably adds emotional tone or nuance to a verbal text that would have to otherwise be elicited through wording and phrasal composition, making it much more efficient and direct than verbal delivery.

Although these canons are found, of course, in all kinds of traditional texts, it is also true that they are inherent in emoji competence. When we told the informants that their messages could be analyzed rhetorically, every single one expressed surprise. After telling them how to analyze their own texts, though, they realized that, indeed, the underlying purpose of using emoji, as one informant typically put it, was "to make the message effective in meaning and style." This statement can, in fact, be adopted as a general principle of emoji usage, as will be elaborated upon throughout this book.

The emoji code

The emoji code is now both a universal and a culturally sensitive system of pictorial communication, given the many reactions and changes that have resulted since its broad usage after 2010. However, as we have seen throughout the first three chapters, there are many elements of the code that transcend culture-specific coding. Indirect evidence of this is the fact that we can decipher the above texts much more so than we could (if at all) if they were written in some unfamiliar script. In the latter case, we would require translation into our familiar language; in the case of emoji, this is less crucial.

There are three generic features that define the emoji code and any code, for that matter. The first one is *representationality*. This implies that the signs and the rules for combining them can be used to stand for something in specific ways. In the substitutive text above, the way in which the text was structured represents a picture "birth story" as envisioned by the text maker, much like the picture stories used for children because they are more readable than they would be with words. The overall representational tone of the message is an obviously humorous one, similar to a kind of joke. Even if we cannot completely translate the story into words, we can certainly extract from it its inherent humor and related sentiments. The second feature is *interpretability*. This implies that messages can be understood successfully by anyone who is familiar with the signs and rules of the code used to construct them. In the birth story text, a considerable amount of inferential thinking was required to glean the meaning from the text. However, again, the fact that a meaning can be gleaned in the first place implies that the emoji code is much more amenable to interpretation than would be a natural language code with which we are unfamiliar. The third feature is *contextualization*. This implies that message interpretation is affected by contextual factors, including outside information or points of reference. There is no outside context provided in the birth story text above, other than the explication that it *is* a birth story; but internally within the text it is easy to see that contextualized cultural references (the celebration emoji, for example) point to a birth story. Context is the guide to interpretation.

Clearly, the emoji code used to construct and comprehend the birth story above is hardly to be construed as having universal culture-independent features leading to its interpretability. However, it lends itself to interpretation more so than it would if it were constructed in an unfamiliar language. Some of its images are coded in specific ways, such as the emoji of the older ladies (presumably members of the maker's family, such as aunts), thus conveying an inbuilt set of cultural frames of reference, likely made inevitable by the available repertory of emoji on keyboards, apps, and websites and the culture in which the story is set. This brings us back to the *Always* episode with which we started off this chapter. The event showed that the emoji code is one that is no longer perceived as a simple adjunctive one to enhance the emotive tone of messages, but rather that it is an evolving language that is subject to adaptive change, thus further reducing its universality status. In other words, the ever-broadening contexts in which the emoji code is being used are shaping the code itself along the lines of natural languages, making it more and more sensitive to political and cross-cultural pressures that ensue from its usage.

In other words, the emoji code, like a natural language, is undergoing change that has nothing to do with facilitating communication, but rather with refining it to meet specific demands. It is thus being shaped by the specific experiences of particular communities of users.

Core emoji

Given the outside forces at work in shaping the emoji code, it is now more accurate to say that it is developing a two-tiered system within it—one that is standard for all users and one that provides optional forms according to situation and context. In other words, the emoji code now has a core and an adaptive peripheral component.

The core lexicon is the one that appears on most keyboards or apps and consists mainly of the facial emoji described previously and images for such concrete referents as the sun, the moon, and so on. Even though these are likely to have a universal interpretability, there are still implicit agreements among users as to what they mean according to where they are placed in messages. But their generic forms help guarantee that they will not be subjected to significant modification via contextual pressures. The concept of core lexicon is actually one that exists in the domain of verbal languages; it is one that goes back to the nineteenth-century origins of linguistics as an autonomous science, although it was elaborated concretely by the American linguist Morris Swadesh (1951, 1959, 1971) in the middle part of the twentieth century, using data from archeology and anthropology to determine which words are likely to be universal and linguistically primordial and which ones are, instead, specific to particular languages. Core vocabularies thus provide linguists and anthropologists with a database for inferring what concepts have been useful to humanity since the dawn of its history and what the common set of concepts is from which all languages draw their original words. The idea is that every language will have words for categories of things that are common to life everywhere—words for mother and father, animals, plants, parts of the body, tools, weapons, and so on.

The core lexicon of the emoji code contains signs that are consistent with core vocabularies in general, liberating them from the phonetic and grammatical specifics of different languages, making them (purportedly) more universal. Interestingly, on Swadesh's list of core items, the first ones are personal pronouns (*I, you, we*), demonstratives *(this, that)*, and interrogatives *(who, what)*, which are followed by concepts such as *one, big, small, person, fish, dog, tree, ear, eye, mouth, hand,* and so on. These are also found in the core emoji lexicon as well. But the features of the specific emoji used seem to vary somewhat across apps and platforms. Nevertheless, they can easily be interpreted, no matter what their specific form might be. As such, they attenuate the possibility of variable or culture-based interpretation. The facial emoji, such as the smiley and the sad face, are also part of the core emoji lexicon, even though they are not found on the Swadesh list, perhaps because the naming of emotions was thought by the linguist to be too highly variable or susceptible to the specific experiences and reactions of different peoples (in line with the relativistic type of linguistics with which Swadesh was involved). However, as work on the face has shown (e.g., Ekman 1973) there seem to be words for basic emotions such as anger and surprise across the world (a topic to which we will return later). So, the emoji core lexicon is, in a sense, an expansion of the Swadesh list.

The Swadesh list also contains common verbs such as *eat, drink, kill,* and *fly*. Corresponding emoji ideographs for these verbal concepts are easily obtainable on various websites and on some apps. These are likely to be located a little lower on the universality scale than are the facial signs, thus involving some variation in interpretability; this is so in all likelihood because of their ideographic nature, since verbs cannot be so easily represented as concrete icons. Nevertheless, for many users the world over, they are interpretable in a straightforward fashion. Overall, noun concepts are the easiest to encode into an emoji sign, whereas those conveyed generally with verbs, adjectives, and other parts of speech are much harder to represent visually and standardized as core items. When we showed various verbal emoji to our informants, they showed no hesitation in interpreting them correctly, even though several of them said that they rarely used them.

According to various sources, such as Unicode, there are over 800 emoji characters commonly supported across most platforms. These include mainly core items. As supported by iOS 9.1, there are now around 1,600 signs that are used broadly across platforms, including all regular emoji (such as the facial ones), but also country flags, and various ideographs. The "nonregular" emoji are those that thus require a little more effort in comprehension. So, if we take this into account, discarding some emoji that refer to specific referents (such as flags), then the research team was able to come up with around 1,000 items that can be said to constitute the core lexicon.

Certainly, a more scientific way to determine what is universal and what is not is to conduct a statistical analysis of actual usage, which was beyond the scope of our research project. However, there is indirect anecdotal evidence that the 1,000-item core vocabulary is not out of line with actual usage. The following set of characters is, according to Macworld (http://www.macworld.com), the one most frequently used by iOS customers in 2016. Most of these were determined to be part of the core lexicon; however, as can be seen, there are signs in the set that can hardly be construed as truly universal; it does tell us indirectly, though, that the main users of emoji are likely to be those who speak a European language and, more probably, English, since various signs clearly make reference to the cultures where these are spoken:

Frequently used emoji characters

Incidentally, only a few of these were not included in the 1,000-item lexicon: for example, the ticket stub and wrap emoji above. A perusal of other websites claiming to contain "basic" emoji was also conducted. It was found as well that most of the items fell well within the core lexicon established by the research team.

The peripheral lexicon

To reiterate, the spread of emoji usage across the world is evident from the statistics mentioned at the start of this chapter. On Instagram alone, it is estimated by the company itself that around 40 percent of the posts contain at least one emoji. In some places, such as Finland, the number climbs to around 65 percent. The Finns have also created their own series of national emoji, such as the *sauna* emoji. Trends such as these are leading to the need for more and more diversity in the emoji code leading, in turn, to the emergence of what has been called here a peripheral (subsidiary) lexicon to supplement the core one for specific or specialized communications. This development, as alluded to above, does not, however, impugn the degree of emoji interpretability in any significant way. Even substitutive texts, made up with peripheral items, are more accessible to interpretation than verbal texts composed in an unfamiliar language. Part of emoji competence today is the ability to know when to use the core and the peripheral lexicon in tandem. As one informant in the study for this book aptly phrased it: "We all know how to use common emoji, such as the smiley; but we all use other emoji if we need to, even though they are not always easily available."

It was Loufrani (Chapter 1) who created an online emoji dictionary, which he organized into categories, including separate sections for moods, flags, animals, food, nations, sports, weather, and others. There is no distinction in it, however, between core and peripheral items, likely because these were registered early on, in 1997. Loufrani then made an "Emoticon Directory" available for downloading in 2000; it consisted, interestingly, of 1,000 smiley signs. This might be the first attempt to designate what a core emoji lexicon might look like, even though there was no apparent plan to do this on the website; moreover, there are quite a number of signs in the lexicon that would hardly be considered to have a universal status today.

From the outset, some emoji had a specific meaning, such as the *bowing businessman* and a *white flower* to denote "brilliant homework." It was the Unicode Consortium that saw the emoji code as potentially having universal usage if it were to be modified to highlight the picture-words that had a potential core status. From 2010 onwards, Unicode has in fact developed a standard system for indexing characters, which has allowed not only for emoji usage outside of Japan, but also for users anywhere to decide, *ipso facto,* which ones would likely emerge as universal and others as peripheral. Within this system, emoji are being added on a daily basis to meet specific demands, including new facial emoji, without impugning the core set. With its expanding peripheral lexicon, the emoji code is now capable of meeting the demands of different cultures and different interest groups.

Needless to say, this conjures up the specter of ambiguity (Chapter 2), suggesting that there is now a duality in emoji competence (universal and peripheral). The *nail polish* emoji, discussed previously, is a case in point. It appears to have a universal value, but it has evoked (and continues to evoke) different reactions, given its rhetorical symbolism with models of femininity that are not universal. However, the original smiley set has rarely been challenged or even questioned by people across the globe.

Unexpectedly, both the core and the peripheral lexicons have brought about problems in interpretability. The reason is that the pictures can develop different overtones and connotations depending on the language and culture of the user. When we asked an informant of Middle Eastern origins who had escaped his country because of turmoil a few years back, what the smiley might mean to him and his family back home, he pointed out that "it is difficult to use smileys when you are constantly suffering and fear for your survival." In fact, he tended to use emoji less than others and did so only if the message was truly enhanced in some way. Therefore, even the use of core emoji can differ from user to user. Also, because emoji can be used as nouns, verbs, or other parts of speech, when they are strung together or distributed in some way, it tends to be the structure of the user's native language that guides their selection and distribution. So, one might find an adjectival or verbal emoji at different positions in a message just as one would with words in different languages, depending on who created the text.

Interestingly, since the emoji code is now the unofficial second language of virtually anyone with a computer or mobile device, a database of both core and peripheral emoji forms and syntagms now exists that is used by the Keymoji function found on iOS keyboards. This is an autocorrect software that translates words into appropriate emoji. As one types a message, the Keymoji software can figure out what the intentions of the user are likely to be, turning them into picture-words automatically. One can now also upload individual emoji translations for any word or phrase, and this will be added to the user's personal database.

Compression

The emoji code allows one to deliver nuances of meaning in more compact and holistic ways, vis-à-vis the longer sequential elaborations required in alphabetic writing. In other words, it displays the quality of compression—which can be encapsulated with a colloquial saying—"a picture is worth a thousand words." More specifically, the emoji code is an economical system for rapid communications, allowing for an enhancement in meaning that would require much more linguistic material, so to speak, in alphabetic writing.

Efforts to make communication rapid and economical have existed throughout history. For example, in the seventeenth century, Louis the XIV wanted to standardize alphabetic forms with the imposition of the *roman du roi* typeface, developed by the Academy of Sciences to map the typeface onto a grid, as opposed to previous typefaces which had developed in a random fashion over time and which were hand cut. This was, however, a move to give the king control over writing systems and thus to imprint his stamp of authority into literacy practices. The standardization of emoji into a core lexicon has several commonalities with this. In this case, the authority is not regal, but technological and commercial. On the one hand, a uniform or core code is likely to facilitate and guarantee that senders and receivers essentially "speak the same language," but in order to do so they must have the same hardware and keyboard, and this is where technocratic forces come into play. Those who wish to expand the code for reasons of a culture-specific or commercial nature, have to petition Unicode or other "technological authorities," which will decide if the petition is valid or not, much like a king would have done in the past. If it is deemed to be useful and even necessary, then Unicode will translate the request into emoji that can be read across delivery systems as part of its ever-expanding peripheral lexicon.

King Louis's project failed, given the complexity of the typeface choices that his move entailed. In a parallel way, Unicode's standardizing ability has its own limits—emoji are fonts and thus cannot be displayed uniformly across devices and, more importantly, emoji users are constantly modifying and creating them through ingenious manipulations that fall outside the Unicode system. This topic will be broached again in subsequent chapters.

Given its holistic nature, pictorial communication was already a tendency in common everyday communications before the advent of emoji, including the use of computer icons, visual signs in public places, commercial logos, and so on and so forth. So, in a sense, the "modern eye" was already accustomed to processing pictorially encoded information. The emoji phenomenon is an outgrowth of this intrinsic tendency in communications. In a world where brevity and rapidity have become basic interactive values—the shorter the message the better—the emoji code emerged right on time, so to say, to allow for a delivery of messages in a compressed, rapid, and effective way.

The critical reactions against this type of writing are, actually, predictable. Any time that a shift in writing and (more broadly) literacy practices occurs, there is a tendency to view it as disruptive and indicative of a decline in "standards." This is actually an ancient mindset vis-à-vis the role of writing in the practices of knowledge making. Actually, writing emerged to replace orality in this domain, and this itself was cause for concern. In his *Phaedrus*, Plato ironically inveighed against the threat of writing as impacting negatively upon memory and diminishing the ability of the mind to detect inconsistencies of logic in rhetorical expositions. Plato was afraid that written speech was far too instrumental, able to persuade people simply because it was non-dialogical, and thus did not allow for a back-and-forth repartee that attenuated, if not eliminated, the danger of manipulation. Of course, contrary to Plato's fear, writing spread and became the very basis upon which knowledge was constructed thereafter. The striving for more rapid, brief, and "to-the-point" writing, rather than the protracted style of treatises and philosophical disquisitions, has become a major tendency in modernity. Mass communications technologies have always been geared toward achieving this goal. Compression is a term used by cognitive scientists (Alexander 2012; Turner 2012) to refer to the process of condensing large amounts of information into compact forms. There is no doubt that the emoji code achieves compression through its basic pictographic nature.

There have been various attempts before emoji to construct compressive visual symbols in communication and representation.

Among the most famous are the symbols of Charles Bliss, which will be discussed in the final chapter, and the shorthand notation system of Sir Isaac Pitman, created in 1837:

Sir Isaac Pitman's notation system

Pitman's system had a stenographic purpose, that is, it was intended for recording oral dictation or discourse quickly. All stenographic systems are meant for professionals, and were used mainly before the advent of recording devices such as tape recorders. They require specialized training; emoji writing on the other hand does not, even though one must become familiar with the code before actually being able to use signs effectively. So, emoji are much more than abbreviated picture-words to be used by professionals; on the contrary, they are not likely to be used by professionals, but by anyone aiming for rapidity in communication (like stenography) and wishing to imprint emotive nuances in their messages.

4 EMOJI SEMANTICS

We must think things not words, or at least we must constantly translate our words into the facts for which they stand, if we are to keep to the real and true.

OLIVER WENDELL HOLMES JR. (1809–1894)

A 2015 study by Novak, Smailović, Sluban, and Mozetič has indirectly provided a statistical substantiation of the main theme elaborated so far in this book—namely, that the emoji code is used primarily to enhance the positive tone of an informal message. The researchers analyzed 70,000 emoji-containing tweets in thirteen different languages, finding essentially that positivity in tone is the main function of the basic emoji code. As they concluded: "most of the emojis are positive, especially the most popular ones." The study ranked 751 emoji on a scale with three main points: *positive, negative,* and *neutral.* The scale was designed to identify the "neutrality level" of any emoji. Overall, the researchers found that the main intent of emoji was to add positive nuances to the content of texts, no matter what their intent or purpose.

Adding nuances of specific kinds is the basic semantic objective of emoji usage. The term semantics is used here to refer to the meaning of any sign or sign form and the structural aspects connected to it, such as its location in a text (Morris 1938, 1946). Not all codes possess semantic structure. Alphabet systems, for example, do not—unless, of course, a specific character is taken from the code for specific symbolic reasons, such as the use of the letter A to mean "excellence" or X to stand for "anonymous signature," among other meanings. Alphabets provide the materials (the signifiers) for building words and other meaning-bearing structures. On the other hand, like other pictographic systems, the emoji code possesses intrinsic semantic structure—that is, the emoji refer directly to concepts, emotions, and so on either adjunctively, substitutively, or in a mixed fashion (as we saw in the previous chapter). Alphabet systems possess double articulation, which implies that they provide a limited set of characters with which to make complex forms ad infinitum (Martinet 1955). Many codes possess this type of structure, including digit systems, such as the decimal and binary ones. Emoji, instead, possess presentational structure, to use Suzanne Langer's (1948) term—that is, they possess meaning inherently.

The main difference between emoji and full-fledged pictographic systems of writing is, as mentioned previously, that they are used mainly in an adjunctive way, although there is a rise in their substitutive uses, as we shall see in subsequent chapters. Emoji are also different from historical pictographies in that they are constructed beforehand and thus chosen from a preset repertory, such as that found on a keyboard. So, they have a hybrid structural value, so to speak—that is, they are, in part, like alphabet characters which are chosen to construct larger structures such as words; and, in another part, they are pictorial forms that have presentational structure. As such, they provide a wide array of semantic nuances to written texts. As far as can be told, they are never used in formal writing contexts or to express something serious or grave. They are attempts by individuals today to diminish the danger of potential conflicts stemming from communicative encounters. One informant emphasized to the research team that "I would never put an emoji on an essay; I would probably fail it, if I did." Another one declared that: "Emoji help me make my message positive, avoiding conflicts even when I have something bad to say."

As Jean Petitot (2010: 1016) has aptly observed, the notion of semantic structure being adopted here "essentially refers to the system of connections which organically link up parts within an organized whole." As is well known, Saussure (1916) referred to the structural make-up and meanings of signs as based on the relations they had to each other (Bouissac 2010). Basically, a structural semantic analysis of emoji involves examining them as connected to the other parts of messages, that is, as part of the ways in which messages are constructed, framed, and presented.

This chapter will focus on the semantics of the emoji code. Perhaps the increasing use of emoji and other visual signs in internet communications is going to change how alphabet-using cultures will eventually reshape or modify their writing practices. If so, a primary reason is that visual-presentational forms of writing have an intuitive appeal. Emoji may in fact be leading people to retrieve an ancient form of "visual consciousness" that was evident in the origins of writing, as discussed in the opening chapter. The rise of visual-iconic communication in digital media may, on the other hand, be a temporary and thus passing trend, as will be discussed in the final chapter. In future forms of communications, alphabetic writing may once again regain its hegemony, especially if voice-activation technologies become more widespread, thus reducing the need for informal written communications such as texts and tweets. But, at present, this is not the case. We asked the informants in the research project: "Which form of communication do you prefer among friends—written (as in text messages), F2F, or through some screen or device (such as Skype)?" Remarkably, virtually everyone answered that the written medium was their preferred one, mainly because the other media were more fraught with potential dangers. As one informant observed referring to text messages that she sent to her parents: "Texting allows me to make sure we don't fight, as we often do when we talk to each other."

The thesaurus effect

The term emoji was used mainly at first in reference to the core facial icons described in previous chapters. Given the emergence of a peripheral lexicon, today the term implies images of all kinds, including those of objects, people, and events. As we have seen, emoji have both pictographic and ideographic representational structure. But because they do not involve the requirement of drawing each form individually at the time of usage, which entails highly variable and subjective modes of construction, they are unlike the early pictographs, which were drawn by individuals on surfaces, revealing the subjectivity of the pictographer (Sebeok, Bouissac, and Herzfeld 1986). As mentioned, emoji are selected from a standardized set available, like alphabet characters, on many keyboards or apps today. They can be supplemented by various additional apps or online sites that make them easily accessible. So, the semantic nuances are already implicit in the prefabricated signs themselves. For example, the emoji below enfold, *grosso modo*, the same meaning built in advance into them, as we have already seen. They are repeated here for the sake of convenience:

Smiling emoji   Winking emoji   Heart-eyes emoji

All three stand for the same emotive referent—happiness. But the details of each face add specific kinds of nuances to this meaning. The smile and half-lunar eyes of the left-most emoji conveys the intended meaning as unambiguously as possible. The middle one communicates the same emotion, but it does so with the addition of a wink, indicating some relationship with the interlocutor—that is, it adds a secretive or perhaps jocular nuance of emotionally pertinent meaning that exists between interlocutors. In the emoji to the right, the mouth is more open and the heart-shaped eyes are intended to increase the intensity of the emotion, implying that there is a romantic intent or relationship involved between the interlocutors. The lack of eyebrows puts the focus even more on the eyes. So, while the basic semantic intent of each emoji can be easily seen in all three, the different details in facial representation add semantic nuances that shape their ultimate meanings, and these tend to have a cultural coding effect. So, for instance, the winking emoji would hardly be considered acceptable in cultures where romance is not allowed to be given public or individualistic expression. In all three emoji, therefore, the meaning nuances are derived from the configuration of the mouth, eyes, and eyebrows; this is what adds the nuances to the overall usage of the forms.

Moreover, these meanings are distributed in a text in an organic fashion—that is, they do not simply decorate it; they are part of its meaning structure. The left-most emoji appears typically as a message ender in most of the 323 texts analyzed, generally in place of a period, assuming the phatic function of making a brief message endearing, rather than abrupt, as would a punctuation mark (as already discussed). If either of the other two is used in endings, however, this phatic function is intertwined with a specific emotive one (romance), implying a higher degree of intimacy among the interlocutors and a cue to continue the conversation at a later point. This was found in five of the texts. The emoji with the heart-shaped eyes also has a rhetorical function, conveying affection through the symbolic meanings associated with the heart symbol. The kinds of nuances built into the different emoji can be said to produce a "thesaurus effect," which can be defined as the implied, potential set of related cultural and symbolic concepts that are evoked by an emoji as it is used in some specific context. This effect can be seen, for instance, in the fact that the left-most emoji can also stand for "it has been a pleasure to talk to you." The middle one can also stand for "just a joke" or the innuendo "this is a secret we share," among others. And the last one connects happiness with love and romance in a symbolic fashion. Overall, the three emoji enhance the positive tone of a message, either in a straightforward fashion or else through the various nuances just discussed.

The study with which we started off this chapter (Novak, Smailović, Sluban, and Mozetič 2015) provides the relevant experimental details substantiating this basic semantic model of emoji. As mentioned, the researchers analyzed 751 emoji (in thirteen languages) as to their sentiment value (emotivity)—positive, negative, or neutral. An emoji that is widely viewed as neutral, like the *yin* emoji, is located in the middle of the sentiment scale, indicating its high degree of neutrality. The researchers called their ranking system "Emoji Sentiment Ranking," claiming that it determines the sentiment score (degree of emotivity) of the 751 core emoji. The team enlisted the native speakers of the thirteen different languages to rate the emoji. From their ranking system, the researchers were able to determine which emoji, such as the *crying cat* one, evoked a negative sentiment, and which ones evoked positive and neutral ones. Surprisingly, they found that some emoji, which might seem to have a neutral status, were actually perceived as having a negative value. These included the *straight line mouth* emoji, the *police officer* sign, and even the *bento box*. Although the researchers did not deal with the issue of cultural coding, it is likely that these values might be due to a culturally based thesaurus effect.

The overall conclusion drawn by the researchers is that most emoji are intended to produce a positive sentiment. They also found that emoji tend to occur at the end of tweets, and that their sentiment polarity increases with the distance from this location. Incidentally, the most positive emoji picked by their informants was a vertical line made up of small dashes, which produced a 0.96 sentiment score (the maximum was 1.0). Our own research team presented a similar set of emoji to our informants to rate accordingly, from negative and neutral to positive. We found similar patterns to those in the above study, but we also discovered that the negative ones identified by the study were not interpreted in that way by our informants—strongly suggesting the presence of a culturally based thesaurus effect. With regard to the *bento box* emoji, for example, all the informants expressed surprise at its purported negative value. One informant put it as follows: "Maybe those speakers live in countries where it is a 'bad' symbol for something; it looks OK to me."

Framing

The use of emoji to create a specific tone and, thus, the interlocutor's frame of mind to a conversation, is part of what Erving Goffman (1974) called logically "framing"—the presentation of concepts from a particular perspective so that it can be "framed" through the forms used. In alphabet-only communications, the sender's frame of mind must be extracted from the distribution of the words and phrases and in how they are selected strategically. This requires quite a bit of cognitive effort and language-based know-how, including very specific semantic-pragmatic knowledge, associated with the discourse practices, in tandem with the semantic and stylistic structures of the language used. It is often the most difficult feature to present in communications among speakers of different languages, because it is embedded in the semantic and syntactic organization of verbal messages. In emoji-using texts, on the other hand, the framing of one's perspective is easier to do, via the choice of visual tokens, with their inherent nuances, that are more comprehensible across languages than are those encoded by words. The framing is also rendered much more comprehensible because it involves the placement of the icons at strategic points in the message. So, for instance, when irony is intended—perhaps the most difficult aspect of framing in written languages—it can be much more easily communicated not only in the actual facial structure of an emoji, but also where it is placed in the message. The wry smile on the *cat face* below is interpreted broadly as giving an ironic tinge to a message, as we discovered from the informants in the research group; significantly, it accompanies phrases such as "You get my meaning, don't you?" or "Just a joke:"

Ironic cat face

This emoji conveys a frame of mind that is assumed to be universally understood—a feature called equivalence framing. But this is not necessarily so, since irony typically entails the use of verbal contrasts within conventionalized discourse practices that can only be understood through familiarity with them in cultural contexts. The above emoji is essentially an "emphasis frame," which highlights the features of irony in a visual way, not only in the configuration of the face, but also in the choice of the cat metaphor itself, which is used in many pop-culture domains, such as cartoons and comics, where the animal is portrayed commonly as a clever and sardonic creature. Thus, the emoji is part of a network of meanings in a specific culture that, in tandem, can be activated to produce ironic nuances. The framing of irony is vastly different in cultures where the cat does not bear these cultural connotations. Nevertheless, when we asked the informants if they would use the above image with people from non-English-speaking cultures, such as with the friends they have in other parts of the world, almost everyone said that they probably would, but that they would accompany it with other emoji that are less culture dependent in order to "explain" it. Most were convinced that "internet-savvy" interlocutors across the world would easily pick up the intended irony, because they are being constantly "engaged," as one informant aptly put it, in a networked world.

In a similar analysis of graphic elements in multimodal internet environments, Johanna Drucker (2014: 155) makes the following relevant observation:

> Erving Goffman's frame analysis is particularly relevant to the processing of a web environment where we are constantly confronted with the need to figure out what domain or type of information is being offered and what tasks, behaviors, or possibilities it offers. . . . In a networked environment, such as an iPhone for instance, the literal frames of buttons and icons form one set of organizing features. They chunk, isolate, segment, distinguish one activity or application

from another, establishing the very basis of expectation for a user. Engagement follows, and then returns to the interface in an ongoing process of codependent involvement.

It is certainly true that emoji-based framing seems to heighten the engagement and codependence of interlocutors, perhaps even more so than in any other context. This type of analysis, actually, goes somewhat contrary to the classic study of verbal conversations in the mid-1970s by Paul Grice (1975), which portrays the codependence as guided by conversational maxims that govern all human interaction. Grice assumed that communication required the ability to attribute mental states to others and thus to anticipate the verbal forms in people's minds that described these states—that is why, purportedly, people understand each other. Although he argued that context played a role in shaping the framing process, in the end he claimed that the purposes of communication were to exchange information. But the semantics of emoji suggests that information in a denotative sense is rarely, if ever, involved in a speech situation. The emotive-rhetorical nuances built into emoji-containing messages cannot be pinned down to a set of information-transfer principles. The 100 student informants were asked to indicate the relevance of using emoji in message making. Ninety-two responded that they would never use emoji in an angry message or when discussing something serious, thus indicating that emoji have a strictly contextualized emotive function, rather than a purely informational one. However, if the relevant situation should arise, they pointed out that they would use emoji to help make a difficult message much more digestible, so to speak.

Connotation

The thesaurus effect involves connotation, applying to all emoji, not just facial ones, to higher or lesser degrees. Consider the emoji below, which were used in four of the 323 texts examined:

Four-leaf clover   Strawberry   Van/Minibus   Clock/Time

The four-leaf clover implies a particular connotation ("good luck"). It was used to wish an interlocutor good luck for an upcoming test. The strawberry icon was employed to indicate that the interlocutor liked to eat it during periods of stress. The van/minibus was used after the phrase "This is how my parents get around," with an obvious ironic intent. The clock icon was used after the expression "Time is ticking" to indicate that an important and inevitable event was fast approaching. In other words, the choice of the icons involved much more than conveying information or sprucing up the written text visually; rather, they added specific connotative nuances to its meaning, most of which were derived from culture-specific symbolism. Connotations cannot be checked or tamed in any usage of signs by humans. They are always present and, according to some semioticians, are even the basis upon which our common ideas and concepts are formed and utilized.

In semiotics, two main forms of meaning are recognized as operative in all signs—denotative and connotative. Denotative meaning is the one built initially in a sign so that some referent, such as a *van* (above) can be distinguished from some other vehicle. It has, more technically, paradigmatic meaning, whereby it is a selection that can be made from a set of similar items. When considered as a separate word or emoji, the word *van* has denotative value. However, when used in a context, such as a text message, the *van* sign carries with it a whole array of connotations that come from its previous social and cognitive uses. Connotations are, again more technically, part of syntagmatic structure. When a word or emoji is used with other structures, it takes on connotative value. This is not an option, as some traditional literalist theories of semantics continue to sustain to this day; it is something we are inclined, or indeed even impelled, to extract from signs as they are combined and used with other sign forms.

The emoji semantic system is intrinsically connotative and, some might say, even poetically so to a degree. The *heart-shaped eyes* emoji discussed above brings out how this type of connotation works. When found within a text, it instantly compels one to process it as if it were a visual-poetic symbol. The heart symbolism is an example of the poetic function of communication, in the sense that it has a poetic-emotive style and value. Peirce (1936–58) called the purely denotative aspect of a sign's referent the "immediate" object, and he called the many connotations that it evoked its "dynamical" objects. So, the heart-shaped eyes emoji, not only encodes an immediate object (happiness ensuing from romance), but dynamical objects, such as the feelings associated with "heart-felt" romance through the poetic form in which it is presented.

Of course, emoji can be selected to serve primarily denotative functions, especially in contexts where ambiguity and connotative meanings are potentially misleading. For example, the pointing finger emoji, which replaces an actual pointing finger, has mainly indexical denotative meaning:

Pointing finger emoji

Nevertheless, even such a sign cannot be totally constrained to denotative reference, since those who see it may add their own connotations to it, such as "it's about time," "it's too late," and so on, depending on the context. Connotation is also built into the emoji forms standing for personal pronouns (*I, you, he, she,* etc.) and personal names, which are used traditionally to identify persons in terms of their ethnic, familial, and other types of identity background information (Ingram 1978). There are no "pronoun" emoji, as such. So, the "I" pronoun is generally rendered by the picture of a person, as we saw in the "birth story" analysis of the previous chapter. The "you" pronoun is typically conveyed with a pointing arrow, emulating how we use fingers to point out our interlocutors in F2F. And "they" is represented with a group emoji (consisting of various people). So, even though these have the same kind of indexical denotative function of the verbal pronouns, the fact that they involve a creative use of pictures means that connotation is involved. While this may be true of any kind of semantic system, as some theorists would maintain, it is *especially* and *invariably* true of emoji semantics. It is relevant to note that a new type of emoji, called "bitmoji" has surfaced to represent identity. The image can be selected from a set on a keyboard or an online venue, thus influencing perceptions of identity in the search for an image that best represents us.

Bitmoji

When we asked the informants if they used bitmoji, many said that they did not because they were a bit "creepy." Basically, it is an app that allows a user to turn himself or herself into an emoji and this, some said, is really not needed since "my friends know who I am and what I look like," as one informant put it. So, the bitmoji repertory may be a passing trend, but its emergence still implies that in the emoji system certain verbal forms are hard to realize denotatively. One informant pointed out that "Bitmoji just turn you into a cartoon character." This may, of course, be appropriate in humorous contexts, but not in others.

In summary, emoji become communicative signs not in and of themselves, but because we imbue them with meaning through symbolism and for communicative purposes. As Sonja K. Foss (2005: 150) aptly observes, this entails a three-part process: "Not every visual object is visual rhetoric. What turns a visual object into a communicative artifact—a symbol that communicates and can be studied as rhetoric—is the presence of three characteristics. The image must be symbolic, involve human intervention, and be presented to an audience for the purpose of communicating with that audience."

Facial emoji

As mentioned at various points in the previous discussion, emoji became widespread at first as replacements of the graphic emoticons for expressing an emotion that is associated with a specific expression in F2F communication. As such, they originated to represent facial expressions in written text through iconic visual images. For this reason, it is useful, if not important, to examine the emoji standing for facial expressions in a more in-depth fashion.

The psychologist Paul Ekman (1985, 2003; Ekman and Friesen 1975) was among the first to study the "grammar" of facial expression, creating an "atlas of emotions," with over ten thousand facial expressions, that is now used broadly by scientists, semioticians, and even the police. His goal was to identify the specific biological correlates of emotion and how they manifest themselves in the configuration of the parts of the face, drawing at first on Darwinian models of facial expressions and relevant research on how facial forms, such as the smile, involve specific reactions. Crucial to his methodology was, in fact, the development of techniques for measuring muscular movements that generate facial expressions. In various combinations, these determine the meaning of a particular expression. From this, a standard set of units (which Ekman called *microexpressions*) can be cataloged and studied for consistency and variation across cultures. One of his findings has been that the basic emotions (disgust, fear, anger, contempt, sadness, surprise, happiness) activate the same microexpression patterns across the world, within statistically predictable variation. Perhaps the reason why we react universally to the meanings of the basic facial emoji is that they incorporate the main microexpressions in stylized outline form.

Ekman's findings are not uncontroversial—some researchers claim to have found that emotions are in large part learned, rather than innate. However, Ekman's findings seem to have an intuitive validity beyond these critiques, since he also discovered a high level of cross-cultural consistency in the facial presentation of basic emotions through a series of studies with diverse members of Western and Eastern literate cultures. It is no coincidence that among the first emoji that became used broadly across the globe were those standing for these very emotions—whether or not their constructors had read Ekman's work or came independently to the same conclusions:

Anger	Disgust	Fear
Happiness	Sadness	Surprise

Emoji for the basic emotions

A perusal of real faces will show a remarkable consistency between the emoji and the faces at the level of microexpression. Ekman eventually expanded his paradigm of cross-cultural primary emotions to include amusement, contempt, embarrassment, excitement, guilt, pride, relief, satisfaction, pleasure, and shame—all of which are reproduced in emoji form as well. Without going into Ekman's procedures for eliciting facial expressions, and his specific findings vis-à-vis cultural variation, it is sufficient to say here that his research suggests the existence of a core set of universal facial expressions. So, it should come as no surprise to find that the semantics of the face, so to speak, is intrinsic to the core emoji lexicon. Needless to say, there is probably significant culturally based connotation as to what the emoji mean; but at a denotative level of expression, there is little doubt as to what emotion they are referring. It is at the connotative level of meaning, of course, that these are interpreted via cultural templates.

Ekman started his research project in the 1960s, establishing the Human Interaction Laboratory in the Department of Psychiatry at the University of California at San Francisco in 1963. He was joined by Wallace V. Friesen in 1965 and Maureen O'Sullivan in 1974. Over the years, Ekman and his team have identified certain facial expressions as universal and others as culture-specific (Ekman 1976, 1980, 1982, 1985, 2003; Ekman and Friesen 1975). In other words, facial expression is a hybrid modal system, akin (remarkably and likely coincidentally) to many scripts. Of special relevance to the present discussion is Ekman's breakdown of facial expressions into details of eyebrow position, eye shape, mouth shape, nostril size, and so on. In various combinations these determine the meaning of a particular expression. As alluded to above, these constitute outline signifiers in emoji facial images.

The general study of bodily signs is called *kinesics*—first developed by the American anthropologist Ray L. Birdwhistell (1952), who analyzed slow-motion films of people interacting during conversations noting that specific bodily actions and reactions surfaced typically in them. He adopted notions from linguistics to characterize the patterns, believing that these actions formed meaning-bearing units that were similar in function to the phonological, grammatical and lexical units of language. For this reason, the system of nonverbal signs studied in this way came to be called (and continues to be called) "body language." Kinesic signs, or *kinemes*, as Birdwhistell called them, can be innate (involuntary), learned (voluntary), or a mixture of the two. Blinking, throat clearing, and facial flushing are innate (involuntary) signs, as are the above basic facial expressions. Laughing, crying, and shrugging the shoulders are examples of mixed signs. They may originate as instinctive actions, but cultural rules shape their structure, timing, and uses. Winking, raising a thumb, or saluting with the hands are learned (voluntary) signs. Logically, their meanings vary from culture to culture. This is perhaps why many kinesic emoji are understood in terms of cultural meanings, rather than as universal forms. The kinesic emoji below of a gesturing hand stands for either "hello" or "good-bye" in imitation of a common salutation gesture involving a waving hand:

Waving-hand emoji

Other emoji for bodily actions, functioning as cultural kinemes, are the clapping hand sign to indicate applause and the open hand sign to convey "acceptance":

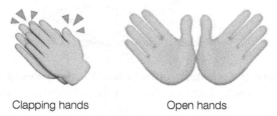

Clapping hands   Open hands

Again, these signs certainly can be seen to refer denotatively to specific manual actions involving seemingly straightforward meanings, but their ultimate interpretation involves cultural coding. Clapping, for example, is interpreted as a sign of approval or praise, especially after some performance in Western and other cultures; but this does not apply, for instance, to some cultures (such as tribalistic ones) or after ritualistic performances anywhere. Similarly, the open hands have a wide array of semantic connotations from agreement to a prayerful meaning that need not concern us here.

There is one last aspect of Ekman's research that is relevant here, namely that certain microexpressions are the result of lying. Meyer (2010) and Heussen, Binkofski, and Jolij (2011) have confirmed that pupil dilation occurs in deception, as is colloquially believed, although the degree will vary considerably from culture to culture and according to the nature of the lie. This means that, by and large, lies can be tracked, measured, and recorded in the structure of microexpressions. One must be careful, however, in visual representations of lying, as Johanna Drucker (2014: 26) has cogently pointed out, because drawing the face "exemplifies a specific method of producing interpretive knowledge and social consensus in and through graphic representations." Thus, rather than constituting straightforward representations, they could easily be interpreted as caricatures. This is true of the emoji that have been constructed to convey lying. The most common is the elongated nose that derives from a culture-specific reference—the children's story of Pinocchio; and this certainly has no basis in the microexpression of the face; it can only be interpreted through cultural connotation. Another emoji has a more microexpressive basis to its outline; it consists of uplifted eyes looking askance thus suggesting deception of some kind:

Pinocchio emoji   Uplifted eyes emoji

In summary, the semantics of facial emoji is the meaning system that has, perhaps, the highest locatability on the universal scale, because of its consistency with the actual findings on the microexpressions associated with the basic emotions. This is certainly the main criterion why these are intrinsic to the core lexicon. Even so, connotation cannot be eliminated from their usage, as has been discussed several times.

Blending

In a fundamental way, all emoji are "metaphorical pictures." Metaphor, as understood today in cognitive science, is not a simple rhetorical device but a conceptual process whereby separate domains of meaning are blended to produce new forms of meaning that amalgamate the various referential domains into one image. So, in a cognitive or neuroscientific sense, emoji can be characterized as blends. For this reason, it is useful here to take a brief digression on blending theory.

The founding work is traced to George Lakoff, Rafel Núñez, Gilles Fauconnier, and Mark Turner (Lakoff and Núñez 2000; Fauconnier and Turner 2002). Lakoff is the originator of so-called *conceptual metaphor theory*, which he developed initially with philosopher Mark Johnson in their now classic 1980 book, *Metaphors We Live By*. The book described a model of how the mind purportedly generates and comprehends language. It does so, essentially, through a process of association that reveals itself in figures of speech, which are tokens of how the mind transforms embodied experiences into abstract concepts that have a manifest figurative structure. Thus, a simple metaphorical utterance such as "That linguist is a snake" is really a token of a blend, connecting people and animals cognitively—namely *people are animals*. *People* is called the target domain and *animals* the source domain. The former utterance ("That linguist is a snake") is a common linguistic metaphor; the latter (*people are animals*), on the other hand, is a conceptual metaphor (CM).

It can be expressed by an infinite set of linguistic metaphors: "My friend is a gorilla;" "She is an eagle;" "Your brother is a squirrel;" and so on. Interestingly, each one provides a different "connotative portrait" of personality, which means that linguistic metaphors are, themselves, derivatives of the more general conceptual blend. The choice of *snake* from the *animal* source domain, produces a basic personality concept. However, if we want to refine our metaphorical portrait, then we can construct derived metaphorical concepts that allow us to zero in on specific details of personality:

1 "He's a cobra."
2 "She's a viper."
3 "Your friend is a boa constrictor."

In so doing, we are thus able to modulate our descriptions of personality in ways that parallel our sensory reactions to each type of snake. This suggests that what are called *domains* in CM theory are themselves products of the process of sense implication—the target domain *(personality)* implicates a specific kind of source domain *(animals),* which, in turn, implicates certain subdomains *(types of animals)* which, in their turn, suggest other subdomains *(types of snake),* and so on. The domains are not autonomous regions of human mentation. They are linked through sense implication. They are "refined blends." Needless to say, one can easily envision how blending works in emoji use. Indeed, if the snake metaphor were implicated, the tendency would be to simply accompany it with the generic snake emoji:

Snake emoji

However, if connotative nuances were needed, then, as the informants pointed out, they would search for types of snakes on emoji apps and websites. If one cannot be located, then they pointed out that they would actually use the relevant verbal metaphor to accompany the snake emoji (viper, cobra, etc.).

Suffice it to say here that the number of significant and corroborative research findings that CM theory has engendered since 1980 has provided a rather substantial empirical platform on which to develop blending theory. As Lakoff and Núñez argued in 2000, blends are not specific to language, but to all forms of cognition. While the claim might seem to be far-fetched, it really is not, especially if we assume that language and systems such as mathematics are cognitively interrelated.

The original designer of emoji, Shigetaka Kurita, took inspiration from weather forecasts that used symbols to show weather and from manga that used stock symbols to express emotions, such as a light bulb signifying inspiration. One can easily see blending processes at work in the origination of the emoji code, which presents visual forms that are pictographic amalgamations encoding various connotative meanings (the thesaurus effect above). Blending can, in fact, be used to describe how the features on a face or image are connected to produce the meaning. Consider the following two emoji:

Sadness   Contentment

The emoji on the left, consists of a specific blend—slouched eyebrows + open mouth (colored in salmon pink) + tears; and the second one of another blend—smile + direct-looking eyes (stare) + crinkles on the smile + female hair. These features, when amalgamated, produce the meaning of each emoji. Of course, these are defined (blended) by the companies who make them available. And this is a crucial part of emoji semantics, as mentioned. The blending process is based on generic models that are assumed to be universal. After being incorporated into Apple's iPhone, Android, and similar apps, emoji have accrued unexpected meanings, because the blending processes vary cross-culturally. Moreover, the exact appearance of emoji is not fixed, as discussed, but varies between platforms or devices, in the same way that normal typefaces do. For example, the Apple Color Emoji Typeface is proprietary to Apple, and can only be used on Apple devices. Different computing companies have developed their own fonts to display emoji, some of which have been open-sourced to permit their reuse. So, for example, the snake emoji above varies in app and media styles as follows:

Apple iOS   Old android   New android   Twitter

Device-specific emoji for snake

Blending thus occurs at different levels. At the micro level, it inheres in the composition of signifiers to form an image; at a macro level, it inheres in the way the parts coalesce to produce metaphorical constructs associated with the image. The operation of these two blending levels can be seen clearly in the emoji below:

Beer   Coolness   OK   Bomb

At the micro level, these are essentially logographs, translating words into images directly. But at the macro level, they embody metaphorical meaning. The "refreshing beer" image to the left shows a typical beer glass (in Western culture) with a frothy foam overspill that conveys the notion of "gusto" or "enjoyable." Some elements of the blending process are potentially universal, such as the color of the beer; but others delve into peripheral meaning domains and would require knowledge of the culture of beer drinking. A similar culture-specific macro-blending process occurs in the other three: *coolness* = blend of elongated letters + sky blue coloring + square contour; *OK* = symbol of agreement or acceptance in the finger configuration + rotundness of the hand indicating pleasantness; *a bomb* = bomb explosion seen as disastrous + dark color of the bomb. Without going into details here, the point is that these embody meanings in specific blendings of the parts.

Consider the heart emoji, a symbol representing an expression of love, as in love cards given at Valentine's. In the message below, it is interspersed throughout to reinforce its affective-romantic content effectively:

Text message-2

The heart emoji is a nonverbal metaphor resulting from a cultural blend—the association of the heart with romance. Lakoff himself has always been aware of the connectivity between figurative language and other expressive and cultural forms, writing as follows: "metaphors can be made real in less obvious ways as well, in physical symptoms, social institutions, social practices, laws, and even foreign policy and forms of discourse and of history" (Lakoff 2012: 163–64).

Each sign can be seen to be a specific manifestation of a CM in visual form. Here are a few examples.

1   *Hugging Face:* is the metaphor for a "virtual hug," reflecting the CM *love is a binding force.*

2   *Thinking Face:* this is a contemplating metaphor, structured in such a way that it resembles the facial microexpression assumed in some cultures to convey thoughtful consideration, implying that one will get back to one's interlocutor with an answer.

3   *Face With Rolling Eyes:* The rolling eyes face is a metaphor for condescension, boredom, or exasperation. It is the verbal equivalent of "Duh" and similar exclamations. The relevant CM is *the eyes are the mirror to the soul.*

4   *Zipper-Mouth Face:* This is an obvious visual equivalent of the metaphor "Zip It," meaning do not talk.

5   *Nerd Face:* This is a slang metaphor visually translating the term "nerd," a foolish or loathsome person who lacks social skills or is

insipidly studious. The buckteeth and the eyeglasses are signifiers that designate this meaning visually.

6   *Slightly Frowning Face*: The frown face is a metaphor through which one can convey partial sadness and hopelessness.

7   *Upside-down Face*: The upside-down metaphor translates the meaning of an expression such as "My life is upside down" with all its blended meanings such as life in disarray, in disorder, in a mess, in chaos, and so on.

8   *Robot Face*: This metaphor visually translates the idea that someone's messages are like those of a robot—repetitious and predictable. The CM is *the mind is a machine*.

9   *Sleuth or Spy*: The spy metaphor conveys the sense of being a little sneaky. The hat, monocle, and cigar at the side of the mouth form a prototypical portrait of the classic detective look.

10 *Speaking Head in Silhouette*: This emoji is used to encourage someone to speak out, or to become involved in a rally or a protest.

11 *Sign of the Horns:* The horn sign has a variety of meanings depending on culture, varying from the "rock on" salutation of urban culture to the cuckold sign of some Mediterranean cultures.

12 *Raised Hand With Part Between Middle And Ring Fingers*: Also called the "Live Long and Prosper" Vulcan Salute from *Star Trek*, it first appeared in the *Amok Time* episode. It was popularized by Leonard Nimoy, who played Spock, and was inspired by the *kohanim*, the Hebrew word for priests, who held their hands during a benediction, with the gesture representing the Hebrew letter Shin.

13 *Dark Sunglasses*: This is an obvious metaphor translating the connotations of the word "cool." This idea has a long figurative history that need not concern us here.

14 *Lion Face*: The lion with a timid face turns the usual fierceness connotation associated with the lion image on its head, in line with the friendliness function of emoji.

An early classificatory framework of visual metaphors is the one by Santaella-Braga (1988), which built implicitly on the work of Group μ (1970)—a group of scholars and scientists interested in the rhetorical structure of all signs. Visual metaphors are powerful because they can be used both independently as single emoji distributed in specific ways, as we saw, to enhance meaning; or else they can be used exclusively to create new kinds of visual meanings.

The power of images

Colloquial expressions such as "the power of images" and "a picture is worth a thousand words" are actually rather useful in providing an interpretive frame for the emergence of emoji and why they are so intuitively powerful as modes of modern-day informal writing. In his 2001 book, *Media Unlimited: How the Torrent of Images and Sounds Overwhelms Our Lives,* Todd Gitlin decries how the modern media provide a constant barrage of visual images that wash over audiences but which accumulate in groupthink to influence worldviews and lifestyle behaviors. "Images," he states, "depict or re-present realities but are not themselves realities" (Gitlin 2001: 22). We know the difference, but we prefer the virtual to the real—a point made as well by Jean Baudrillard (1983), who referred to this blurring of the line between reality and imagery as the simulacrum effect. But the power of images over words is actually a perfect moniker for the origins of writing itself, as discussed previously, rather than just a product of modern technologies. There has been no culture, across time and space, without visual writing traditions and customs. These bear witness to the fact that visual thinking is just as crucial to human understanding, if not more so, than verbal cognition. It is true that we live in a visual culture, as Gitlin maintains, where the image is much more predominant than the spoken word. But this is an oversimplification. Human cultural life has always involved visuality to larger and greater degrees. The problem is that the balance between the visual and nonvisual may have crumbled under the pressure of visually based communications.

While alphabetic writing also involves the use of visual-graphic elements, such as punctuation marks, it is the inability of written text, in the majority of instances, to align the symbols with a specific tone or intended interpretation, with the constant danger of intended meaning not being apprehended, that makes the emoji system a powerful one, overcoming the inadequacies of phonetic writing in this domain. This is not, however, solely an invention of the modern digital world. It existed as well in the writing practices of the medieval and Renaissance periods when manuscripts were illustrated with images of all kinds—called "illuminated texts"—not only to illustrate certain concepts but, like emoji, to enhance their meaning.

Last Judgment, ca. 1440

Although this may be somewhat of an imaginative stretch, it seems plausible to say that the emoji style retrieves a certain sense of the writing styles of the medieval scribes. There are many differences, of course, between the two, which need not concern us here. But the intent seems to be somewhat similar—both use visual forms to give their texts more emotive-poetic power. This was also recognized by Saussure (1916: 10), when he wrote that: "Men might just as well have chosen gestures and used visual symbols instead of acoustical symbols."

Picture writing (pictographic, ideographic, etc.) is often considered to be foundational for human civilizations, since it is the first instance of how written knowledge can be transmitted to subsequent generations independently of the oral channel, thus creating a continuity of knowledge. And, it may also have been the original form for evoking laughter, derision, and satire. The graffiti found on public (square) walls throughout the ancient world, with messages that were politically critical or simply obscene, were usually accompanied by visual supports. Many historical linguists have actually used graffiti as sources for reconstructing languages and the cultures of the eras that the languages reflected. This type of hybrid language (written and visual) has been more the rule than the exception. It could well be that the rise of emoji is essentially a retrieval of this hybridity in writing styles—a topic that will be examined in the final chapter.

5 EMOJI GRAMMAR

Like everything metaphysical the harmony between thought and reality is to be found in the grammar of the language.
LUDWIG WITTGENSTEIN (1889–1951)

The "birth story" text of Chapter 3 required quite a bit of emoji competence to decipher, not only because of the thesaurus effect of the separate emoji, but also because a large part of the decipherment involved inferring the meanings of emoji syntagms, which were strung together in specific ways. In other words, in addition to semantic aptitude, knowledge of emoji grammatical structure—the rules or practices that govern how emoji are sequenced in syntagms—is clearly an intrinsic part of emoji competence.

Like any natural language grammar, the distribution of emoji in texts, as well as the construction of phrases and sentences with emoji symbols in them, implies a systematic structure, otherwise it would be impossible to literally "read" the emoji texts. In some, such as adjunctive ones, it is fairly easy to see how the system works, as we have seen throughout the previous chapters—an example is the placement of a smiley in the endings of texts as a substitute for a period and for the final salutation (for the semantic and communicative reasons already discussed). In other words, emoji grammar is often nothing more than a "placement grammar," based on calquing, or the superimposition of emoji in slots where verbal structures would otherwise have occurred if the text were written entirely in words. However, in some texts, there is a different system at work, whereby the sequencing and compositional aspects are governed by conceptual aspects, rather than strict rules of grammar. In such cases it is obvious that there is a pictorial-conceptual grammar involved. A large part of the birth story, in fact, implied the use of this kind of grammatical structure, allowing the emoji sequences to tell a story through a conceptual-pictographic layout. Calquing and conceptualizing often overlap in some emoji texts. The point is that emoji grammar is not just a replica of linguistic grammar with visual symbols; it has its own "syntactics," or system for organizing the emoji to create coherent and meaningful sequences or combinations.

The goal of this chapter is to look at the characteristics of emoji grammar. Knowing how it works is as much a part of emoji competence, as mentioned, as is knowledge of emoji semantics and pragmatics (to be studied in more detail in the next chapter). Indeed, as in natural languages, the intertwining of the semantic, syntactic, and pragmatic dimensions of the emoji code allows users to engage in the cognitive flow of text and thus either to produce or comprehend its meaning.

Calquing

To see what calquing involves, consider a few examples from the mobile game called "Guess the Emoji" which tests people's emoji competence in a jocular way, by presenting a string of emoji that aim to translate into pictorial form popular song lyrics, citations, proverbs, and so on. In other words, the emoji translations are calques involving the superposition of emoji forms onto the syntactic layout of the word forms. The examples below were provided by a member of the research team, who found them on the game's website. They are emoji versions of: (a) the title of a famous American song ("Singing in the Rain"), (2) a cosmetic treatment ("Bikini wax"), and (3) a type of clothing ("Bomb shell bikini"):

Singing in the Rain   Bikini wax   Bomb shell bikini

Examples of emoji calques

In (1) the microphone emoji stands for "singing" and the umbrella-rain drop emoji for "in the rain"; in (2) the bikini emoji is superimposed on the spot where the word "bikini" occurs, and the painful emoji face is a conceptualization of the word "wax," indicating the reaction to waxing, rather than the word itself; and (3) the bomb, shell, and bikini emoji are put into the same sequence as the words in the phrase "bomb shell bikini."

The emoji sequences follow the verbal sequences exactly, mirroring their syntactic layout. Of course, conceptualization is involved in all three, since the mirroring is not an emoji-for-word one, but rather a pictorial-concept-for-word one. The calquing is thus not purely lexical, but also involves conceptual and rhetorical dimensions.

Calquing is, thus, more precisely a "transliteral" process, whereby the words in verbal expressions are converted to emoji (picture-words) that are grounded in a pictographically based conceptual system. A reader who knows the emoji system can thus easily reconstruct the original words; one who does not will find it very difficult to do so. Calquing is also involved in the placement of emoji in typical informal messages, as discussed in previous chapters. In this case it is more substitutive and purely semantic (through the thesaurus effect) than in the case of transliteral calquing, where figurative mechanisms are involved (a topic that will be discussed subsequently). This kind of calquing occurs at the end of messages, and more generally, at the end of thoughts as they occur in messages. As we have seen, these constitute emotive punctuation marks that make a message positive in tone and overall effect.

Clearly, as even a cursory consideration of how emoji are placed in texts or in how they transliterate verbal texts, there is a system involved. Entire phrases and sentences constructed with emoji are dependent on this autonomous system more so than in transliterations. This means that the syntactics of emoji in a string or syntagm involves both calquing and conceptualization—that is, they occur in a semiotically logical order. As we shall see in the next section, however, this does not mean that the syntactic flow of verbal sentences is eliminated; rather, it means that it is blended with the pictorial-conceptual syntax of the emoji code.

Conceptualization

The spread of emoji-only texts is probably a consequence of the growing practice of using emoji in marketing, branding, in political campaigns, pop culture, and so on, all of which is, according to some, a transparent strategy for communicating with the younger generations, as well as for staying *au courant* with the latest communication platforms. As these types of texts become more frequent, then the rise of emoji grammar as a kind of "second-language grammar" will increase accordingly. Like learning a second language via immersion among its speakers, so too learning the emoji grammar involves usage with other "speakers" of the language. As emoji texts spread throughout the social landscape, knowledge of this grammar is also expanding and developing its own conceptual structure. A perfect example is PETA's (People for the Ethical Treatment of Animals) 2014 mobile-based campaign calling for social action against the mistreatment of animals. The campaign was known, rather appropriately, as "Beyond Words"—a moniker that applies to emoji use in general. It featured texts created entirely with emoji. Texting a heart emoji back to PETA would have allowed the viewer to sign up for mobile alerts and become part of a Twitter campaign. Below is one of the original texts used in it:

PETA emoji campaign

The message begs a young woman (the left-most emoji) to think or reconsider (shown by the thought cloud above her) that the things she might wish to buy (dress, shoes, purse, lipstick, boots), laid out in that order to become a "princess" (the right-most emoji), are all animal products and thus destructive of animal life for purely casual lifestyle reasons. Although this is not stated directly, it certainly is implied by anyone who understands emoji grammar and, of course, the referential domain where it is used (the animal rights movement).

As can be seen, reading this message requires more than just knowledge of the semantic possibilities of the emoji. It also requires knowledge of how the forms are combined and laid out and, thus, how these are connected to each other conceptually. This aspect raises several immediately obvious issues vis-à-vis the relation between the text layout and the message. First, conceptual texts of this kind require significant referential background knowledge and a particular frame of mind. Not everyone who sees the text will, in fact, make the association between the products and animal killings; nor does the text take into account the fact that everyone across the world buys such products. In other words, the contextualization of this text is embedded primarily in urban western culture and its purported reckless materialism. More specifically, it seems to be aimed at a specific demographic—white, young Anglo-American-European women. As some critics of the campaign have pointed out, this is a rather stereotypical portrayal of womanhood, and highly restricted to commercial cultures.

Leaving these problems of culture-based decipherment aside, all of which may diminish the impact of PETA's message, for the present purposes it is relevant to note that entire messages can be created with emoji alone, skipping the alphabetic textual part because the grammar of the code is self-sufficient being based on the relation of concepts to each other and to the outside referential domain, rather than on internal rules of sentence formation which guide the flow of thoughts in a sentence. In other words, emoji grammar is not subject to the syntactic rules of English or some other European language. Rather, it has its own "iconic-conceptual" structure, much like pictographic scripts that allow for a direct iconic connection between the forms and their referents. The final thought unit in the text is the emoji for "princess," which is the point-of-arrival of the message; that is, it starts with the image of a young woman and, through the layout of products, aims its message directly at the metaphorical image of women as princesses. The layout of the products is intentionally random, providing the subtext that "it doesn't matter which of these are important to you, they are all made from dead animals." The conceptual-iconic grammar here can be seen to follow a three-part ordering, much like the Subject-Verb-Object (SVO) syntax of most sentences in English and European languages.

1   a young woman thinking about or desiring to purchase = the subject of the sentence;

2   beauty-enhancing products = the implied verb of buying the products;

3   to become a "princess" (the object of the sentence).

Therefore, the emoji-constructed sentence, although conceptual, still has a basic verbal syntax guiding it: that is, the sentence layout from left-to-right follows the syntax of English grammar. The positioning of (1) to the left, as in a typical subject slot in a declarative sentence, assumes unconscious knowledge of how the actor-agent relation unfolds; indeed reversing the first and last emoji would create a meaning dissonance or asymmetry. According to some cognitive linguists, this type of conceptual structure characterizes all of language, unconsciously. Langacker (1987: 7) summarizes this perspective as follows: "Linguistic expressions and grammatical constructions embody conventional imagery, which constitutes an essential aspect of their semantic value. In choosing a particular expression or construction, a speaker construes the conceived situation in a certain way, that is, he selects one particular image (from a range of alternatives) to structure its conceptual content for expressive purposes."

Langacker has even argued that the parts of speech themselves originated through the imagery content of words, most of which is obscured by the way we write them—phonetically rather than conceptually. Nouns, for instance, encode the image schema of a region in mind-space. A count noun such as *leaf* is envisioned in our minds as referring to something that encircles a bounded region, and a mass noun such as *water* a non-bounded region. Now, this difference in image schematic structure induces grammatical distinctions. Thus, because bounded referents can be counted, the form *leaf* has a corresponding plural form *leaves*, whereas *water* does not (unless it is used metaphorically as in *the waters of Babylon*). Moreover, *leaf* can be preceded by an indefinite article (*a leaf*), *water* cannot. Emoji grammar allows for these imagistic-conceptual units to be expressed overtly. Indeed, by simply repeating the same image, pluralization is implied conceptually, even if grammatically the pluralization of a specific form is prohibited. There really are no grammatically acceptable ways to pluralize the word *happiness*, unless we take some leeway with the rules. But in emoji writing this happens all the time, as can be seen by the repetition of the smiley face at the end of the phrase "A maid, a butler, a cook, and a gardener," provided by one of the informants. While this may also mean "very happy" it still constitutes a repeated form that has the same kind of function of pluralized forms in verbal language:

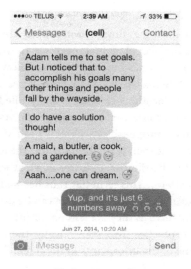

Text message-3

The three money bags can be interpreted as having conceptual pluralization structure; that is, they pluralize "money bag" ("money bags") and have, at the same time, what linguists call an anaphoric function (referring back to something in the text), indicating that getting a maid, cook, and gardener costs money, thus spotlighting the situation in emotive ways. These meanings could hardly be captured by a single character or grammatical form in natural language, or even by words or phrases in the same emphatic way. It is relevant to note that the 323 texts analyzed for this project and the many online texts compiled by the research team show that emoji grammar is developing its own syntactic forms and markers to carry out common grammatical functions, such as pluralization. So, while calquing is connected to specific linguistic forms via transliteration, conceptual grammar reconstructs the syntactic flow of sentences (such as the SVO one) into a conceptual assemblage; this induces emoji users to organize their texts according to the nature of the concepts, albeit in line with the syntax of the language they are using.

Syntactics

To summarize the foregoing discussion, the insertion of emoji adjunctively into texts is systematic, occurring at points in the sentence or paragraph that are intended to bring out some emotive, phatic, or poetic aspect of the meaning. In substitutive texts, the concepts encoded by the emoji guide the overall textual meaning. In this case, too, a form of syntactic calquing occurs, whereby the emoji follow the same syntactic flow of corresponding verbal texts. In both types of texts the emoji are superimposed in locations that are usually filled by specific kinds of words, punctuation marks, or parts of speech. As such, they reflect an internal "syntactic propensity" whereby both their meanings and sentence grammar guide their textual allocation. The term used to refer to this propensity in the distribution of forms in a text was called syntactics by Charles Morris (1946). This term has thus been adopted here since it implies that the meaning of some structure can be determined only as it relates to other structures as they are laid out or ordered in texts.

To grasp what syntactics involves, consider the message below that was provided by one of the informants in the research group:

Text message-4

This message includes a GIF referring to an office worker who has been through a difficult period—GIF is an animated clip that is attached to a message. The smiley face with the tongue sticking out (repeated eight times for emphasis) comes at the end of the sentence, "im gonna make her yell at u so u flip," replacing both the normal period mark, and adding humor as a means for the other interlocutor to laugh at the situation. If the emoji were put at the start of the sentence, this effect could hardly be achieved since the emoji would precede the thought expressed in words. In other words, there is a kind of dynamic interaction between the syntax of the English sentence and the conceptual syntactics of the emoji—that is, the latter are congruent with the syntax to produce the cognitive flow of the message.

This kind of syntactic organization would have been inconceivable in any form of previous alphabetic writing practices. If images and diagrams were incorporated, as in a scientific paper, the purpose would have been for illustration or elaboration. Indeed, in formal writing such as science papers, visual supports such as charts, diagrams, models, and so on are part and parcel of the writing style. But they are hardly calques or syntactic conceptualizations. However, these too are located at specific "thought points," where they not only illustrate or summarize some theory or empirical finding, but often shed light on it. So, while the two forms of writing styles may seem different, there are some points of contact between them. Both exemplify a hybrid writing style, as it has been called in this book.

As the message below shows (provided by another informant), this type of dynamic interplay between the iconic content of emoji and the syntactic structure of the language used is providing a highly effective form of strategic writing style. The type of reading that is involved in deciphering the text is very much a hybrid form of understanding—a form that is characteristic of rebus writing which is based on a combination of pictures and words:

Heyyy Yvonnnne! 💚 Thank you sooooo much for the time and effort you've put in for me these days! I really can't thank you more 🙏 🙏 and thanks so much for paying all those little things for me I'm so sorry I forgot to pay you back in person last night 😕 😌 😢 what's your bank and what's your email address? I'll just transfer you back!! I'm super duper glad that I could meet up with you after omg 17 years 😂 😭 😭 😌 Im so happy that we get to become closer during my stay in Toronto and I believe we will definitely meet again soon and I'm sure it wont be another 17yrs man. Sorry for not letting you have time doing your school work which makes you super stressed, hopefully this msg could kindly serve as a morning reminder for you to study haha lol Thank you so much Yvonne, you are so kind and friendly and passionate about taking me around and introducing your great frds to me and all that stuff. Good luck on your project and don't stress out I'm sure you'll be fine and you've got this!!! 🙏 Looking forward to seeing you next time soon 😭 😭 😭 😌 😌

Text message-5

The decipherment of the text is, in fact, akin to solving a rebus puzzle since it involves trying to understand where the visual images intertwine with the written text to produce the meaning. The two hearts inserted right after the salutation allow the reader to get a foretaste of the tone or emotional subtext of the message—basically it alludes to an expression of affection, thankfulness, or tenderness. It is a visual exclamation point, both reinforcing the "Heyyy Yvonnnne" salutation, and adding the nuance of affection directly into the salutation. The location of an emoji after the verbal salutation is typical of most of the text messages examined by the research team. Its post-verbal-salutation collocation seems to indicate, generally, both reinforcement to the tone of the salutation, and a way of conveying friendly intimacy and bonding.

The two facial tears emoji allow the receiver to literally see the emotional aspect of the gratitude being expressed for her generosity. In this case, the collocation is a semantic calque, since it comes right after "can't thank you more," thus immediately reinforcing the verbal expression of gratitude with its facial counterpart. Three of the remaining emoji insertions come at the end of a sentence or phrase and thus function to bring closure to each sentence's main content. All three are syntagms:

1 cross-eyed face + flat-eyes face + angry face
2 sweating face + two heart-eyes faces + ironic grinning face
3 three kissing faces + two heart-shaped-eyes faces.

The insertion of (1) occurs at a point where the interlocutor wishes to emphasize her own foolishness in not paying her friend back. The emotive progression in the syntagm from cross eyes to flat eyes and finally to an angry face indicates an increase in the degree of anger or displeasure at herself for not taking the appropriate action—the cross-eyed emoji starts the emotional cascade (so to speak) by implying that she does not understand how she could have forgotten to pay her back; the flat-eyes emoji is an admission that she regrets having left the scene without repayment; and the angry face emoji completes the cascade to indicate that she is upset at herself because she forgot to pay her friend back or perhaps that her friend did not remind her about payment. The insertion of (2) after pondering that it was seventeen years of friendship that was at stake reinforces the perceived importance of the friendship itself—the sweating face likely indicates the strong emotional bond the sender feels vis-à-vis the friendship; the two heart-eye faces indicate the extreme happiness she still feels with regard to the friendship; and the ironic face conveys the emotion of incredibility at the length of time that has passed. The insertion of (3) as a closing part to the message is a summary syntagm conveying the strong friendship the sender feels for the interlocutor. Finally, the "strong arm" emoji inserted before the final sentence is a book-end image with (3), since both allude to the strength of the friendship.

The above conceptual syntactics is typical of all kinds of emoji texts. From the remaining 322 messages collected for this book the same type of distribution of emoji was observed—that is, the insertions were: (1) *syntactic*, inserted at locations where punctuation markers or salutation formulas occur or co-occur; (2) *semantic*, inserted to represent some meaning emotionally at the spot in the sentence that this meaning occurred; and (3) *reinforcing*, that is, inserted to reinforce some verbally indicated meaning. Emoji grammar is thus governed by utterance meaning, rather than purely textual meaning. A summary of these features of emoji grammar in the text messages is charted below. The numbers refer to actual occurrences, not to specific messages. So, if in a message there were five syntactic emoji, in a second one six, and so on, the method used to compute the total number of such emoji was simple addition (5 + 6 +...); the same procedure was used for the semantic and reinforcement emoji. Moreover, the identification of an emoji as having a syntactic rather than a semantic function is purely practical. As discussed, these overlap considerably. So, for the sake of clarity, a syntactic emoji is one that is placed at the beginning or end of verbal structures, often in place of punctuation; a semantic emoji is one that is interspersed in the message next to any word or phrase to annotate the meaning; and a reinforcement emoji is one that illustrates or reinforces some verbal meaning:

Syntactic	Semantic	Reinforcement
1,615	1,938	878

The conceptual-iconic syntactics of emoji grammar conforms somewhat with general theories of visual writing and thinking (Arnheim 1969; Dondis 1986; Saint-Martin 1991). However, because emoji are chosen from a digital set of options, they are unlike other visual syntactic systems, as we shall see in the final chapter. Now, the question arises:

Does the same grammar apply to texts that are written entirely with emoji? As we saw above, an ad like the PETA one does indeed have a conceptual grammatical structure, whereby the layout of the text follows the grammar not only of sentence formation but also of conceptual formation. One of the most interesting examples of texts written entirely with emoji comes from a book by the artist Bing Xu titled *Book from the Ground: From Point to Point* (2014). The following excerpt from Xu's book shows a message that is constructed entirely with emoji:

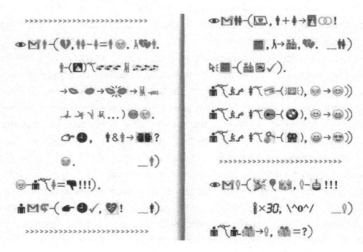

Message constructed entirely with emoji (from Xu, 2014)

Clearly, this type of text requires a rather high level of emoji competence where semantic, syntactic, reinforcement, and conceptual aspects of the grammar interrelate with each other to produce the meaning behind (or underneath) the visual symbols. Translating it here into, say, English is a moot point because it would be an individual interpretation of sorts more than a veritable translation. What the emoji phenomenon is showing, more than anything else, is that visuality and phonetic writing are merging more and more to produce a hybrid language and, thus, that human communication in written form is evolving more and more on a single path of hybridization across the globe, at least on the surface. We are beginning to sense, in other words, that the traditional forms of language and writing are no longer able to carry our thoughts in the ways of the past.

Rebus writing

It is obvious that the decipherment of the Bing Xu text above is exactly like solving a rebus puzzle. It is not the point to do so here, as mentioned, but several features merit commentary nonetheless. First, a starting and ending part is signaled by a series of chevrons (>>>>>>>), much like a section-break in computer texts, and regular punctuation marks (commas, periods, exclamation points, etc.) are used throughout, as are number symbols. These are also similar to computer layouts, such as HMTL script that have specific functions at these locations. In effect, this type of message reveals a high level of amalgamation of scripts, symbols, and various visual forms. It is a form of writing that is based on "combining schemas," to use Cohn's (2013: 28) rather apt phrase with respect to comic-book writing style. Above all else, it involves what has been called above a form of "rebus decipherment."

Rebus writing prefigures emoji writing. It is type of hybrid script that has existed since time immemorial. It is not known where, when, or why it originated. Coins with rebuses inscribed in them, representing famous people or cities, were common in ancient Greece and Rome. During the Middle Ages, rebuses were frequently used to encode heraldic mottoes. In Renaissance Italy, Pope Paul III employed rebuses to teach writing. In the early part of the seventeenth century, the priests of the Picardy region of France put them on the pamphlets they printed for the Easter carnival, so that even the illiterate masses could understand parts of the message. So popular had rebuses become throughout Europe that Ben Jonson, the English playwright and poet, trenchantly ridiculed them in his play *The Alchemist*. Rebus cards appeared for the first time in 1789 (Costello 1988: 8). The gist of this rapid historical foray is that rebuses have been used as part of a strategy to both bolster alphabetic writing and to teach literacy.

It is unlikely that the meanings of entire emoji-constructed texts will ever be easily deciphered uniformly across the globe. And even among interlocutors who share the same linguistic-cultural backgrounds, these are idiosyncratic and require a lot of context in order to be deciphered. The rebus form of writing seems to resist easy decipherment. The German manuscript below is dated circa 1620 (https://commons.wikimedia.org/wiki/File:Arolsen_Klebeband_18_041_3.JPG):

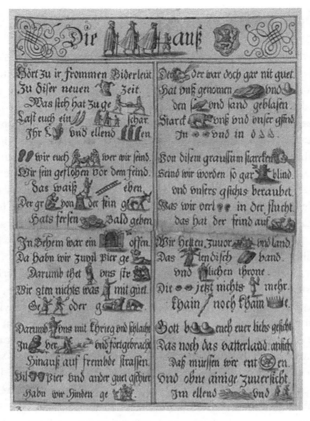

German rebus manuscript

A close inspection of the text will show that the use of images is identical to their use in hybrid emoji texts. In the past, rebus writing was used frequently for comedic and satirical purposes. It was perceived to be subversive by the authorities, who, as a consequence, banned many rebus texts.

As can be seen from the Bing Xu sample above, texts written entirely in emoji symbols require even more effort to decode, like solving very difficult rebus puzzles. They can be said to have a high level of visual noise—the term "noise" is used both in its communications meaning of any interfering factor in the delivery of a message that can obstruct its meaning and in the psychological sense of anything that is overwhelmingly confusing. It is perhaps because of visual noise that entire emoji texts are still rare. None of the 323 texts used for this project were written in complete emoji style. One of the informants put it this way: "Those are too difficult to write and to read; interesting though."

On the other hand, there is the possibility that the exclusive and uniform use of emoji may spread. There are a huge number of emoji-focused projects being created online at present. If realizable, then this is truly a radical paradigm shift in human communication, since it would entail the learning of a new literacy based on emoji grammar. It is unlikely, however, that this is attainable or even desirable given the high level of visual noise that would always be present and likely not eliminated even through familiarity. Each text would be a rebus puzzle and would take too much time and effort to decipher. The written communications among the young people in the research group unfolded mainly as micro-conversations and the emoji were essentially cues that added to the utterance meaning of the messages.

Of course, as we shall see in the final chapter, visual communication does have many benefits, and thus may still guide the rise and spread of the emoji code. One of these is in avoiding reading disorders. Dyslexia is unknown in pictographic-ideographic cultures such as China; it exists primarily in alphabet-using cultures (Shlain 1998). Whatever the neurological reason, it is obvious that emoji can be used as expressive forms for counteracting dyslexic tendencies associated with alphabetic linearity. Perhaps they are even changing the way the brain processes textual information. As Barthes and Lavers (1968: 10) put it, long before the advent of emoji, visual writing entails "the promise of a semiotic relationship between form and meaning that moves past words, and constitutes a relation between images and words."

Perhaps the amalgamation of alphabetic script with emoji into a hybrid code is an evolutionary process that may be spreading beyond its contextualization in informal messages. But, as we saw with the texts above, it is not disruptive of the syntax of the verbal language—that is, the grammatical syntax of the written part is unaltered; it is simply bolstered by the visual signs interspersed systematically (as discussed). Overall, the emerging hybrid writing systems bring out the importance of writing in human culture. Such writing systems are based on the rebus principle. In fact, alphabets themselves arose through the unconscious operation of this principle. The pictogram for "arrow," for example, could also stand for "life," because the same word was used in the Sumerian language. So the sound of the word that starts in both is detached and made into a unit (a phoneme) that can be used over and over in words that possess it. If the arrow sign could stand for both "arrow" and "life," because they are both pronounced in the same way, why not use the arrow sign for the sound itself wherever it occurs, regardless of its meaning? The Sumerian language was made up largely of one-syllable words, so it was not difficult for the Sumerians to work out a system of about one hundred phonetic signs. The hybrid emoji writing system may be an unconscious retrieval of the rebus principle. Deciphering an emoji-containing or emoji-constructed text involves an interplay between the iconic concepts and their relation to verbal language, as we have seen in this chapter.

Overview

The theme here has been to show that emoji are not devoid of syntactic structure. Whether through calquing or through a series of syntactic alignments with language grammar, the emoji system, may, in fact, be having an impact on language itself, forcing people to think imagistically and conceptually, rather than linearly and in terms of the flow of the syntax itself. Moreover, it is becoming ever more obvious that the ways in which emoji are used is subject to variation, as the emoji-only texts show. The same kind of variability started with emoticons, as Terry Schnoebelen (2012) aptly observes:

> People vary in their use of eyes, mouth shape, face direction, and whether or not they represent a nose in the face. And we see these in groups other than smiles—in variants of frowns and winks, for example . . . the variants correspond to different types of users, tweeting with different vocabularies. Emoticons are not simply representations of internal emotional states. They are more interactive in nature, positioning authors and audiences around propositions. The meaning of a given emoticon goes beyond its affective stance. For example, emoticons have variants that have greater or lesser affinities to standard language. Researchers who are interested in style, stance, affect, computer mediated communication, variation, context, and sentiment analysis will find ample grist for their mills.

The same type of analysis applies to the use of emoji. The following three statements made by informants in the research project actually encapsulate this perfectly:

1 "I use emoji like others, but I am also different, because I like to put them in places and in combinations that mean a lot to me; I hope this works with my friends."

2 "I can figure out emojis most of the time; but sometimes I have to write back and ask my friend what she meant; I guess emojis are a lot like words; we use them any way we want."

3 "Many of my emoji are the same as those of my friends; but sometimes I create new ways of using them. But my friends still understand my uses because, I think, they understand my train of thought. It's easier to be inventive with emoji than with anything else."

6 EMOJI PRAGMATICS

All the evolution we know of proceeds from the vague to the definite.
CHARLES SANDERS PEIRCE (1839–1914)

The overriding objective of the creators of emoji is to make written communication between anyone, regardless of language background, more and more possible. But, as we have seen, this has not turned out always to be the case. The use of a yellow smiley was intended to eliminate any potential stereotyping or representational favoritism that would come by using a white or black face. But this has, itself, created pressure to stylize the emoji to reflect racial and ethnic features. As the emoji code becomes more and more shaped by such diversification pressures via usage, it is leading to a new form of communicative competence—a term introduced by linguist Dell Hymes in 1971. With it, Hymes wanted to suggest that knowing how to use language is as systematic as knowing the rules of the grammar of the language being employed. As mentioned previously, knowledge of the emoji code (or any linguistic code for that matter) involves an interplay between linguistic and communicative competence. The latter is also called, more specifically, pragmatic competence.

After examining the 323 texts provided by the informant group and tagging each one in terms of their main pragmatic functions, it was found that most could be assigned to two main categories:

1 *Adding tone.* Since written communication can be ambiguous or unable to present mood or tone, the emoji code provides, as we have seen, a visual means to convey prosodic meaning. The term *prosodic* is used here in the sense of "emotive tone." For instance, saying "sorry I can't go today" is less effective and more emotionally ambiguous than "sorry 😢 I can't go today." The former version

risks being interpreted as conveying a certain nonchalance about being sorry, whereas the emoji version does not.

2   *Injecting a positive mood.* All of the examined texts inserted an emoji at end points in a significant thought unit, to allow for visualization of the mood or sentiment expressed by the writer. Frequent and persistent use of emoji has revealed that a main pragmatic function is to inject an overall tone of friendliness and pleasantness to the message (as already discussed). Of course, when sadness is called for, then the emoji chosen will convey this mood just as effectively. However, the sadness is still embedded in positivity—it is a mood that interlocutors wish to share, not deny (which would make the tone negative by default).

The tone-enhancing function is the most important one. As Lauren Collister (2015) argues, emoji act as discourse particles allowing for potential misunderstandings and threats to be attenuated and even eliminated. When something awkward or offensive may arise, the emoji step in to add inflection that can weaken the potentially conflictual interpretation. It is for this reason that the smiley emoji dominates. In the 323 text messages discussed here nearly 2,000 smileys were found. In the absence of physical tone, which might lead people to read a negative content in a message, the smileys are discourse particles for rendering the tone positive or at least calm and assuaging.

This chapter will look at the pragmatic functions of emoji, some of which have already been discussed schematically in previous chapters. They are given a more detailed analysis here. As we have seen, there is a system of emoji usage that has arisen spontaneously through the usage itself. What has emerged is a code that is becoming more and more "natural," rather than artificial, and thus adaptable to different cultural and pragmatic needs.

Pragmatic competence

Knowing how to employ emoji strategically constitutes a form of pragmatic competence, which implies knowledge of how to "code switch" between alphabetic and emoji writing. It also includes knowledge of how to use animated emoji and GIFs appropriately. A number of the texts examined included a mini video clip in picture format directly showing the feelings or nuances of the tone that the interlocutor wanted to communicate. In certain conversations, the interlocutors just used emoji back and forth, especially when the content and tenor of the textual conversation had become predictable. Some of the GIFs had captions underneath, making the message clearer, and often funnier. Overall, the emoji forms are "mood enhancers," generally imparting, maintaining, or reinforcing a sense of togetherness among interlocutors. One informant made the following relevant remark: "I can always make my messages happy just by putting a happy face in them, even when the news is not good. And this makes me feel united to the person I am writing to."

Knowledge of how to write strategically in the new digital media has become a subject of great interest to linguists and semioticians. Pérez-Sabater (2012), for instance, found similar communicative strategies in her study of writing practices on Facebook to the ones found in the informant texts. David Crystal (2011) has claimed that how society views the new writing, or more accurately, the two new forms of writing (online and offline), each one contextualized according to medium, is having an impact on all kinds of social processes. In schools, it is not uncommon for educators and students to be given the choice to move back and forth between the two literacies. As far as the research team could tell, however, the use of the emoji code is not common in student-teacher interactions. One informant made the following relevant statement: "I would use emoji only with a prof who I know from many classes and who is friendly. I would never use it with my economics prof, for example, 'cause he is too strict'."

What is certainly clear is that the internet has had a direct impact on traditional school literacy, including an increasing use of informal registers, inconsistency in writing patterns, and a rise in abbreviated writing. Naomi Baron (2008) claims, however, that online literacy practices have little effect on offline ones, since the two now exist as a dichotomy, producing what can be called a new kind of diglossia, with online writing being assigned a low (informal) value and offline formal writing a high (formal) value. Others claim instead that online language is a pidginized form that may eventually develop into a global creole that will indeed signal a new form of literacy. Actually, given the fact that emoji use is writing based, it may have actually increased sensitivity to writing itself, thus producing a kind of "meta-literacy" awareness. As discussed, it constitutes a hybrid of phonetic and picture writing, making it much more interesting. Traditional writing is static, but hybrid writing is dynamic both in how words are spelled and how they are supported visually and (sometimes) audio-orally.

Hybrid competence also implies the development of different subliteracies and textual practices, including "mobile pragmatic competence," which implies knowledge of the kinds of texts that can be written on mobile devices vis-à-vis other media such as Twitter, Instagram, or Facebook, where there is an audience rather than a single interlocutor involved. This hybrid competence is thus media-dependent. In fact, there are now media-specific textualities, such as text-messaging poetry and cellphone novels, consisting of chapters that readers download in short installments. The email medium is the one that is closest to traditional print literacy practices. It is the medium used by businesses, schools, and other institutions and is thus more sensitive to formal registers than other types of digital communications.

In this new pragmatic environment there are ever-growing modalities of communication that cut across modes emphasizing a basic use of hybrid literacy—verbal and nonverbal. As Halliday (1985: 82) predicted a while back: "When new demands are made on language, it changes in response to them. . . . We are making language work for us in ways it never had to do before, it will have to become a different language in order to cope." This new form of literacy (textual and visual) also entails vernacular literacy—knowledge of how different languages or jargons now interact—and information literacy—knowledge of how to mine information from the internet and appropriate it for communicative practices. Overall, hybrid literacy can be defined as the ability to extract and use relevant information in multiple formats from a wide range of sources via digital devices. It thus encompasses other literacies, such as technological and information literacies, that go beyond traditional reading and writing skills.

Stark and Crawford (2015) discern a politicizing angle to this new literacy—to convey affect and thus support the current political-social system. In other words, hybrid writing is a way to maintain what Italian Marxist Antonio Gramsci (1931) called cultural hegemony, or control of the masses through indirect means and one of these is writing. The researchers argue that emoji are conduits for "affective labor" in the social networks of "informational capitalism," as they term it. Emoji are thus seen to be rich in social, cultural, and economic significance. Emoji represent emotional data of enormous interest to businesses in the new digital economy, constituting signifiers of affective meaning. The two researchers suggest that emoji forms both embody and represent the tension between affect as human potential and as a productive force that capitalism continually seeks to harness through the management of everyday biopolitics. Emoji are instances, therefore, of a contest between the creative power of affective labor and its limits within a digital realm in the thrall of market logic.

This whole line of reasoning may have some validity, and the appearance of emoji in ads and political slogans may be anecdotal support for this hypothesis. But there was nothing in the text messages examined for this book that even hinted at this potential ideological dimension to emoji, conscious or unconscious. Indeed, when the question of affect and capitalism was posed to the informant group—"Do you think that emoji can be used to manipulate people in a capitalist society?"—virtually everyone answered in the negative. They did point out that the potential for such use was there, but then it has always been a danger in previous forms of persuasive writing.

Emoji are understood as light-hearted, almost comedic forms of communication, but, according to Stark and Crawford, they ultimately have a socioeconomic intent behind them that precedes the range of mobile devices where they commonly appear. Beginning with the rise of the smiley, they maintain that visual language is a cultural form that has emerged out of typographic habits, corporate strategies, copyright claims, online chat rooms, and technical standards disputes. While this aspect to their argument may be disputable, their claim that emoji have morphed into a widespread vernacular discourse, serving to smooth out the rough edges of digital life, is a well-made one. As we have also seen, emoji do considerable work to underscore tone, introduce humor, and give individuals a quick and efficient way to bring some color and personality into otherwise boring networked spaces of text. Yet emoji also do more than this. Beyond their enhancement of tone, emoji can act as an emotional coping strategy and a novel form of creative expression, even if, in both cases, they are constrained by pragmatic-textual conventions (as we have seen). Emoji create new avenues for digital feeling, while also remaining ultimately in the service of their makers.

According to Sarah Ahmed (2010: 29), "affect is what sticks"—to people, places, and objects. Above all else, emoji are exemplary of the tension between affect as liberating human potential, and as a productive force that the market continually seeks to harness through the commoditization of emotional modalities. As Alexander Galloway

(2006: 95) puts it, "it is precisely those places in culture that appear politically innocent that are at the end of the day the most politically charged." Clearly, there may be more to emoji than what literally meets the eye. The concept of emoji arising to serve an economic system, however, is only speculative. What is more relevant is how the emoji code arose in the context of an emerging new global intelligence which has generated its own new knowledge forms. Politics follows on the coattails of innovations in communications and technology; it is the latter that are of primary interest here.

Salutation

The most basic pragmatic function of emoji, as argued throughout this book, is to add emotional tone and to emphasize certain phatic aspects of communication. One of these is salutation—starting and ending messages. It is useful at this point to briefly revisit here the main pragmatic functions of communication, such as the emotive, phatic, poetic, and referential (illustrative) ones before discussing their manifestations in more detail.

As is well known, Roman Jakobson (1960) saw the study of functions as critical to understanding the overall nature of human interaction. He saw them as connected to structural constituents of verbal communication, identifying the following six as the basic ones:

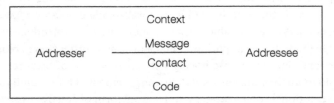

Jakobson's constituents

The addresser is the one who initiates a communication and the message is what he or she wishes to communicate. The addressee is the intended receiver of the message, and the context is what permits interlocutors to decipher the intent of the message and thus to extract an appropriate meaning from it. The mode of contact between the addresser and addressee is the set of personal and social relations between interlocutors that shapes the overall register and meaning of the interaction (as formal, friendly, etc.). The code provides the linguistic and nonverbal resources and cues for constructing or deciphering the message.

Jakobson matched these constituents to six speech functions:

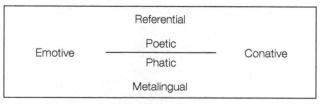

Jakobson's functions

The emotive function correlates with the addresser's intent in constructing the message. The conative function is the effect the message is intended to produce on the addressee. The referential function corresponds to the context in which an utterance is delivered, indicating that the message is constructed to convey specific information about something. The poetic function draws attention to the form of the message itself, producing an aesthetic effect, much like poetry. The phatic function is designed to establish, maintain, or assuage social contact. Finally, the metalingual function underlies messages designed to refer to the code used. As we saw, the term phatic comes from the work of Malinowski (1923), who defined it as the exchange of words and phrases that are important less for their dictionary meanings than for their social functions. When we greet an acquaintance with "How are you?" we hardly expect a medical report, as would a doctor. In other words, it has a pure phatic function, intended simply to allow people to make contact (with a health-wish subtext). Malinowski also argued that the study of phatic communication would allow anthropologists to understand how its varying forms reveal differing cultural emphases and evaluations of what constitutes norm-based behavior.

Salutation is a basic form of phatic communication. In the text messages collected by the research team, it can be seen to regularly overlap with the emotive one (as discussed several times previously). Indeed, in the text messages the traditional salutation of "Dear . . ." never occurs once. Rather, an informal "Hey" followed by an emoji is a common strategy; often only emoji are used. Consider the text below, found on a public domain website.

Salutation emoji

The text starts with several emoji that identify the addresser—all the visual components that are part of the male sender's identity portrait (male face, suit and tie, pants, business shoes, briefcase). Interestingly, the female addressee answers in the same emoji style with her own female portrait (female face, dress, female shoes, and welcoming kiss); and she signs it, not with her name, but with a baby smiley that represents, obviously, their child, followed by child talk ("Da Da"). These have a basic phatic function preceding the relevant verbal statements ("Honey I'm home" and "Welcome home dear"). The conative dimension can be seen in the fact that the female's response involved the use of a family image (the child) that has obvious importance to her and to her husband.

Many examples of phatic uses of emoji were found in the text data collected for this project. A classification according to function of the emoji used in the 323 messages provided by the informants shows how each function manifests itself in actual usage. Note that in many cases the functions overlap, as in the analysis above—that is, the phatic and emotive functions are commonly intertwined in salutations of all kinds:

Function	Actual number of emoji used
phatic	412
emotive	589
conative (= emoji with strong emotional content)	512
referential (concrete referents)	456
poetic	134
metalingual	0

The fact that we could not find a single example of a metalingual emoji is not surprising, since emoji are enhancers of meaning; they are not designed for making statements about themselves. The text below shows how these different functions overlap in message construction:

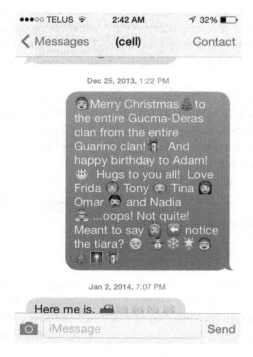

Text message-6

The "bookend" Santa Claus and Christmas tree emoji in the salutation are intended to set the festive tone of the message, synchronizing it as well to the season, much like a traditional Christmas card. The gift package emoji after "the entire Guarino clan!" functions both as an enhancer of the exclamation mark and a referential reinforcement of the overall tenor and theme of the message. The birthday cake emoji is referential and emotive, since it both connects the message to the imagery of birthday celebrations as well as constituting a visual-emotive exclamation mark. The facial signature emoji are identity portraits of the message senders. It is interesting to note that the one who actually composed the message—Nadia—signs herself as a princess, possibly alluding to the fact that she may be the youngest in the family and thus considered to be the princess of that family. Nadia reinforces this conceptualization with her final remark, "notice the tiara?" which is accompanied by the image of a princess with a tiara and an arrow pointing to it. The ending string of emoji summarizes the intent and theme of the message in terms of a rebus syntagm—smiley + snowman + snowflake + star + Santa Claus + tree + bursting star (metaphor for festivities) + gift—constituting a final "season's greeting" salutation. The last set of emoji allow Nadia to avoid ending the message abruptly, intimating the need for continuity between her and her interlocutor.

The kissing face emoji, which is used more commonly between female interlocutors as a salutation particle at the end of a message, is also employed typically in this way, that is, to signal a need to continue the conversation or, at least, to ensure that it does not end abruptly. The text below is a case in point:

Text message-7

The final syntagm consisting of the same emoji repeated four times exemplifies this function clearly, strengthening the phatic force of the salutation. In looking over the 323 text messages of the research sample, it became evident that the salutation formulas of traditional print texts have virtually disappeared. Moreover, it would appear that the specific choice of the final emoji constitutes a kind of signature. The text message data showed, in fact, that a specific sender would tend to end his or her message with the same kind of emoji throughout his or her texts.

Punctuation

As we have seen, emoji have taken on several of the functions of punctuation through calquing. But they also add a conceptual element that is not typically there in traditional script—they mark significant meaning-cuing points in the textual flow. It is relevant to note that the practice of *scriptura continua* (writing without spaces or other marks between the words or sentences) of ancient texts (such as those in Latin and Greek) was reformed with the introduction of punctuation to remove unintended ambivalence and to reduce the effort to process the text (Wingo 1972; Saenger 1997). Between the ninth and fourteenth centuries European texts started to be written with the words separated, presumably because of the spread of early literacy and the need for texts to be read more easily by making the written words correspond to their sequential phonetic composition. Other punctuation marks followed and became standardized after the Gutenberg revolution in the late 1400s, which opened up the possibility of the mass, cheap production of written materials. Scriptura continua is still used in various Southeast Asian languages that use pictography, although modern Chinese languages also use punctuation, borrowed from the West over a hundred years ago.

The punctuation function of emoji allows for what can be called "mood breaks" in the flow of the text and "mood finales" when used at the end of messages. As we have seen repeatedly, the happy face functions commonly as a comma or period in hybrid (adjunctive) messages, adding mood to the breaks. The following messages were taken from the informant-provided sample of texts. In the exchange below, the smiley was used in place of sentence-ending punctuation. In so doing, though, it added significantly to the "love mood" that envelops the whole exchange:

Text message-8

In the text below, the syntagm of faces after "OK," rather than a punctuation mark, allows for a range of moods to be conveyed through the changing facial expressions.

Text message-9

The first emoji in the syntagm conveys a sense of worry, since it involves sweating, while the second one expresses some anger at the information provided (or more accurately at the information that is lacking), and it is repeated at the end to emphasize this mood. The two crying faces add the sense of sadness that the addresser feels. The calquing of emoji as punctuation markers, as such examples show, has made the elicitation of mood a systematic function in hybrid writing.

Other pragmatic functions

There are various other pragmatic functions that require some commentary here, even though, overall, emoji allow addressers to emphasize attitude, mood, and point of view. In the text below, the emoji faces are essentially visual discourse particles that reinforce the various emotional states or moods inherent in the back-and-forth repartee.

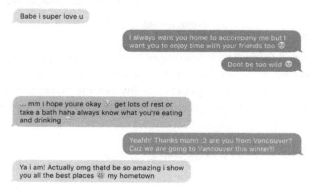

Text message-10

The emoji on top conveys understanding on the part of the addresser that her addressee needs other kinds of friends and, so, that she is happy for her. However, she issues a warning with a winking emoji—a warning not to be "too wild." The wink is a way of communicating that the sender will pretend not to think about the social implications of her friend's departure and interactions with others. The two emoji used in the receiver's response—showing worry and then a knowing wink—manifest a syntactic connectivity with the previous particles thus assuming an anaphoric function, that is, the function of referring to something already stated. Finally, the sardonic grin of the final emoji indicates savvy with respect to familiarity with the city of Vancouver.

An interesting pragmatic function found in the textual data is the conveyance of irony—and in some, cynicism. For example, the "extremely happy" face, 😆, is used often as an ironic discourse particle, similar to a grin for conveying irritation or annoyance at something. In the message below, it is iterated three times and the syntagm is completed with a conspicuously ironic thumbs-up emoji, reinforcing the cynicism experienced over the perceived pointless spending of money. The thumbs-up emoji also functions as a question mark:

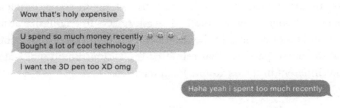

Text message-11

The terrified face emoji is a stronger ironic discourse particle, utilized especially when the sender is highly uncomfortable about something. In the message below, it punctuates the sentiment expressed in the preceding ironic "ha-ha," forming, in effect, an ironic exclamation mark:

Text message-12

The "tongue-sticking-out" face is also an ironic particle, injecting satire or just humor into the content of a sentence or entire message. Note that it too functions as an ironic exclamation point:

Text message-13

In line with the research of Reyes, Rosso, and Veale (2013), who found that irony is a pervasive aspect of various forms of digital communications, even though it is made more difficult to communicate by the absence of F2F contact and vocal intonation, the text data revealed that ironic meanings are gleaned through location and association—that is, through emoji signatures ("you're a loving person" after a bitter text followed by the emoji with a tongue sticking out), unexpectedness (such as throwing in a satirical comment when unexpected: "she said that she was coming, as she always does, btw" with a laugh-out-loud emoji), and repetition (such as using !!!!!! followed by a blend of various emoji after an assertive message).

Another pragmatic function is to require elaboration of some point. The oops or ugh face, for example, is used to convey a need for clarification and a sense of desire, wish, or expectation:

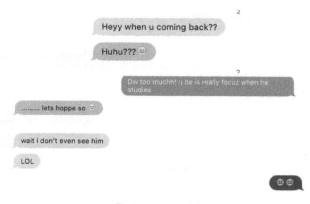

Text message-14

Dismay or disagreement is expressed commonly with the "side look" face, which, unlike a real angry face, is more attenuated or subdued in emotive tone, thus indirectly conveying a desire for resolution:

Text message-15

The upset face is an extension of this function, and it too lessens the negativity in the sentiment by adding a sadness nuance to the message:

Text message-16

The "Oh no" face also conveys dismay, perturbation, or consternation but in a different context; it is used when the situation is unpleasant because of some troubling fact or commotion:

Text message-17

The "Oh okay" face conveys a mixture of compromise, agreement, pity, and slight disagreement:

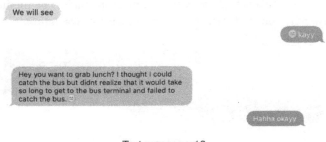

Text message-18

The yelling face is used to beseech clarification or to request a resolution to some misunderstanding:

Text message-19

The "concerned" face, logically, is used to express concern when something is unexpected and the sender has questions about it:

Text message-20

The "sorry" face is used to convey an apology, but it blends the sentiment of pity within it as well:

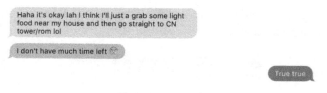

Text message-21

The direct request for pity, however, is encoded in the "tearful" face:

Text message-22

Finally, the "angry" face is employed, needless to say, to convey anger, but not at the interlocutor, since emoji are rarely used in serious-tone messages. It is a visual counterpart to the discourse particle "I don't like it:"

Text message-23

This above exemplification and discussion was meant to show that the choice of words and images in hybrid writing forms an integrated discourse system. Linguist Tyler Schnoebelen (2014) also found similar patterns in the use of emoji in the tweets he examined. For example, the placement of emoji at the end of clauses and sentences has various functions, but it also shows how the verbal syntax connects with the conceptual syntactics of emoji (discussed in the previous chapter). The phrase below (written entirely with emoji) can be decoded essentially as a regret by someone for not being able to meet a partner for a drink:

Emoji phrase

Rearranging the order creates a different story, which seems to be less comprehensible, if at all.

Rearranged emoji phrase

The sequence of emoji indicates a sequence of states or events. The three images below, for example, indicate that sadness precedes a broken heart, which is of course true:

Emoji conceptual sequence

The work of Sacks, Jefferson, and Schegloff (1995) has shown that conceptual structure also governs F2F speech, but less so. There are many gambits that allow for a conversation to unfold in a sequential fashion with implicit structure—that is, as a set of conversational rules that speakers intuitively utilize as they speak. The utterances of interlocutors are thus said to form *adjacency pairs*. So when someone asks something, the interlocutor knows that an answer is the appropriate follow-up in the sequence. Emoji also are used as part of an adjacency system, complementing, reinforcing, and sometimes substituting the verbal part of a message, as we have seen above.

Some relevant questions and findings

The question of whether emoji are used more by females than males came up at several points in the research project. However, there is no evidence that emoji pragmatics is gendered. Indeed, the same kinds of emoji were used equally by the males and females of the research group and for identical discourse reasons. Since the research group consisted of an equal number of males and females (fifty each), there is no reason to believe that our findings will differ significantly in comparison to other similar research projects. In a sense, this new form of communication has "de-gendered" a lot of conversation that has typically characterized F2F discourse. Writing has always had this ability, though, and indeed, unless an author identified herself (as female), it would have been impossible to detect her gender in the writing itself.

The question of politeness also came up in the analysis of the texts. In F2F and traditional writing contexts, politeness cues are used systematically for various social reasons. Using the *tu* (familiar) forms to a stranger in France, rather than the *vous* (polite) forms, would be considered an act of impoliteness or downright rudeness, unless the speaker reveals that he or she is a foreigner either directly or indirectly through an accent. Saying *ciao* ("hi"), rather than *scusi* ("excuse me") to a policeman in Italy in order to get his attention will tend, initially at least, to prompt a negative response (if any). Such forms are perceived as violations in social manners, not as revealing a lack of linguistic knowledge. The cues for politeness in the emoji text data are implicit, rather than overt. Politeness usually involves the use of some friendly facial emoji. Interestingly, Penelope Brown and Stephen Levinson (1987) found that politeness is related to *face*, or the public self-image that we want to claim for ourselves (Goffman 1955: 213). So, that very term in emoji texts takes on a more concrete meaning, since it manifests itself through the selection of an actual facial image.

Although the emoji code is largely restricted to communication among friends and other individuals with whom an informal mode of communication is applicable, it is spreading throughout the internet universe. Twitter communities, for instance, commonly use specific kinds of emoji as their logos. Actually, Twitter constitutes a perfect field laboratory for studying how new writing styles emerge in constrained-usage contexts. In Twitter, as in F2F, there is still a desire to gain the other's social approval and to maintain a positive social identity with the interlocutor. Danescu-Niculescu-Mizil, Gamon, and Dumais (2011) used a system to measure word use in psychologically meaningful categories (articles, auxiliary verbs, positive emotions, and so on). They found that a tweet exhibits a given style if it contains words from these categories. A tweet can exhibit multiple styles and, in fact, the vast majority of tweets do. They also found that tweets belonging to the same conversation are closer stylistically than tweets that do not. Tweeps (users of tweets) who converse regularly are likely to employ a similar linguistic style simply because they know each other or are similar to each other.

As research such as this shows, a connection between the social status of Twitter users and language is established through new styles. By comparing #followers, #followees, #posts, #days on Twitter, #posts per day and ownership of a personal website, the researchers also found that stylistic features appear to be only weakly connected to the traditional social stratification of offline speech. But this might mean that the social status of the interlocutors may not be known. Our research team found that Twitter has become a strategic medium for the use of emoji across the social landscape. The following two are cases in point. The first one was written by Australian politician Julie Bishop and the second one by pop-music star Miley Ray Cyrus. Both were found on the internet.

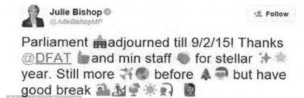

Tweet by politician Julie Bishop

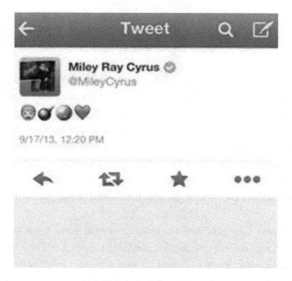

Tweet by Miley Ray Cyrus

The Bishop tweet seemingly uses emoji to indicate to readers that she is *au courant* with the populace, using the emoji as reinforcement discourse particles. All of them have a positive connotative force, implying acceptance, approval, and excellence vis-à-vis her political agenda and activities. Miley Cyrus's tweet implies that she will be successful, that is, she will soon explode (bomb emoji) onto the scene—ending the tweet with a heart emoji to send her love to her readers and to indicate how thrilled she is about her career.

In our interview of the informants, it became obvious that usage of emoji in tweets and other social media messaging is, like their text messages, a means of showing familiarity and connection among interlocutors. They stressed that using emoji is an efficient shorthand method, a fun and entertaining way of communicating a larger meaning in simpler ways. For example, one informant pointed out that his mother would send him a message, while he was away at some peer-based social event, with a set of spying emoji eyes at the start to indicate that she wanted to know his whereabouts:

Spying eyes emoji

Needless to say, the context must be made apparent for the emoji to be interpreted correctly. Indeed, if the above emoji was used between husband and wife, it might have a vastly different meaning, indicating, perhaps, that the sender suspects infidelity or deception on the part of his or her spouse. As the president of *Oxford Dictionaries*, Casper Grathwohl, was reported by the media to have said after an emoji was chosen in 2015 as Word of the Year, the tide has turned, and there is little doubt that the traditional scripts can no longer fulfill modern pragmatic functions:

> You can see how traditional alphabet scripts have been struggling to meet the rapid-fire, visually focused demands of twenty-first-century communication. It's not surprising that a pictographic script-like emoji has stepped in to fill those gaps—it's flexible, immediate, and infuses tone beautifully. As a result, emoji are becoming an increasingly rich form of communication, one that transcends linguistic borders. When Andy Murray tweeted out his wedding itinerary entirely in emoji, for example, he shared a subtle mix of his feelings about the day directly with fans around the world. It was highly effective in expressing his emotions.

7 EMOJI VARIATION

It's different cultures that make the world go 'round at the end of the day.

SAMANTHA FOX (B. 1966)

The upsurge in emoji usage has been made possible by Unicode (as already discussed), the international encoding standard for use with different languages and scripts. Its objective was (and continues to be) to transcend barriers inherent in traditional character encodings, which are largely incompatible across languages. But since 2010, as we have seen, Unicode and other emoji systems are experiencing pressures from across the world for change and expansion of the core lexicon. This has led to the crystallization of variation within the emoji code, shaping it more and more along the lines of natural languages.

Today, users have access to a large variety of icons on keyboards, apps, and websites in order to compose emoji-nuanced (or even complete emoji) messages. This in itself raises the prospect of increased variation, ambiguity, and cultural coding. How would one debate guns in emoji, for example, without avoiding conflictual ideological nuances and interpretations? Moreover, some seemingly straightforward concrete emoji—units in the core lexicon—are themselves interpretable in various ways. When we showed the emoji of an eggplant to the informant group, many laughed and joked that it could easily stand for male genitalia, confirming what many online sites have also claimed:

Eggplant emoji?

Such problems of use and interpretation are the reason why Unicode now allows people across the world to vote on new emoji, becoming a kind of "wiki" system that seemingly democratizes emoji usage and innovation, like the various wikis of the internet. This unfolding situation has obvious implications for the universality of the emoji code. There have been mergers between Unicode and other systems. Unicode has worked, for example, with Apple to add hundreds of emoji periodically to introduce culture-sensitive emoji in reaction to international critiques, and, in fact, many of the new emoji have been designed to represent diversity of all kinds, with skin color options, country flags, and families with same-sex parents. The expansion of the emoji code in this way has necessitated reference materials such as an online *emojipedia,* which keeps track of the additions and provides an overall inventory of the expanding emoji lexicon. Emojipedia has also created a social media campaign called "World Emoji Day," which is held on July 17 each year.

Clearly, the topic of variation is a crucial one in any discussion of how the emoji code is evolving, since, contrary to its original objective of producing a variation-free code, it appears to be developing into a variable code with all the disparities of traditional languages. This topic is investigated in this chapter, which will examine cross-cultural variation and nation-based variation, along with the variation that comes from visuality and internal factors of usage (those that vary according to individuals rather than cultures). Finally, it will look at the cartoon-style literacy that the emoji code promotes and what this implies socially and communicatively.

Cross-cultural variation

As Sonja K. Foss (2005: 150) has aptly put it, even in the domain of visual symbols, variation is inevitable because these "involve human intervention, and are presented to an audience for the purpose of communicating with that audience." In the case of emoji, as we have seen, some of the original ones continue to have a core function, while others are more "audience-sensitive," constituting a peripheral function. The emoji standing for golf or for a hot dog carry with them cultural tags that preclude a standard interpretation. They invariably involve some evaluation of the referent—personal or culture based—that will vary across the world, from positive to negative.

It is for this reason that it is probably not possible to communicate with emoji alone, since as we have seen with emoji-only texts, interpretation is bound to be highly variable (not to mention arduous). The interlocutor needs to know what the sender is talking about, what happened, when and so on, before the emoji sentences can be given an accurate interpretation. It is relevant to note that SwiftKey analyzed more than a billion pieces of emoji data, classified according to language and country. As mentioned previously, SwiftKey is an input method for Android (a mobile operating system designed mainly for touchscreen devices such as smartphones and tablets) and iOS (operating system created by Apple) devices. SwiftKey uses artificial intelligence software systems that enable it to anticipate the next word the user intends to type. It learns from previous text messages and output predictions based on current input text and what it has learned. The results of the SwiftKey study, published online, are absolutely revelatory in regard to the question of variation, since they show cultural preferences and coded nuances in emoji use empirically and concretely. They found that certain emoji were popular in some cultures, but rejected in others. For example, the *poop* emoji is highly popular in Anglo-American cultures and especially in Canada.

Poop emoji

Perhaps this reflects a kind of sardonic sense that can be translated as "the world is shitty no matter what" reflecting stereotypically a supposed Canadian hubris based on ironic stoicism. We asked the research sample, which consisted of Canadian students, about using this emoji and virtually everyone claimed that they use the poop emoji because, as one of them put it, "things stink a lot." The same emoji would hardly have this ironic intent in other countries where public expressions of bodily functions are prohibited. Thus, it might be interpreted in various different ways in these countries, such as: (a) an example of Western vulgarity; (b) an offensive statement; (c) a symbol of corruption in morals; and so on.

The *poop* emoji fits in with the satirical traditions based on indecency, from the ancient satirical plays to the illuminated manuscripts of medieval times. Known as *marginalia*, many of the latter provided sardonic commentary on everyday life, with felines acting like human beings, monkeys, and scatological images (similar to the poop emoji), found throughout this scriptorial practice. The following image is a case in point. It is from an illuminated thirteenth-century manuscript found on the http://www.collectorsweekly.com website:

Illuminated thirteenth-century manuscript

The image suggests flatulence and perhaps excremental functions, similar in ironic meaning of the poop emoji. The smile on the poop emoji actually has a connection to manga—the Japanese comic-book style, where poop is used regularly as part of scatological humor. The point here is that a modern-day emoji still bears within it the embedded historical meanings of isomorphic symbols of the past. This can be called a "transference-of-meaning effect," whereby the meaning of a symbolic artifact remains constant as its form changes over time.

Usage according to nation

The most relevant finding of the SwiftKey project was that people across the world use emoji in specific ways. As our own research team found, and consistent with other studies (Novak et al. 2015), the SwiftKey study discovered that most emoji (over 70 percent) were used to enhance positive and friendly tonality. Here are other findings of the study:

1   In addition to poop, Canadians and Anglo-American societies generally showed a high degree of usage of money, sports, violence-based, and raunchy emoji.

2   Americans in particular used gun, pizza, and drumstick emoji more than anyone else.

3   Australians used emoji referring to drugs, alcohol, junk food, and holidays much more than any other nation.

4   The French used the heart emoji four times more than anyone else.

5   Arabic speakers used the rose emoji ten times more than other language speakers.

6   Spanish-speaking Americans used sad faces more than any other group.

Such findings likely reflect cultural emphases and patterns of symbolism, indicating that emoji may be modern-day forms, but their meanings come from the past—the transference-of-meaning effect. The emoji code, therefore, is being used with culture-specific meanings and attitudes. It is allowing different peoples to evaluate the world as they have in the past, despite the fact that its physical signs are different. While some cut across languages and cultures, there are now many that do not. As Wilson and Peterson (2002) have written, the internet has created new kinds of communities, bringing together dispersed groups of people with shared interests, but retaining their different linguistic and cultural backgrounds. These new communities might be mobilized to further particular political agendas, to bring together dispersed members of familial or ethnic groups, or they might be organized around commodity consumption or corporate interests. But these are nonetheless bearers of traditional symbolic meanings, even though there are definite attempts at keeping the discourse as culturally neutral as possible. The attempt is there, but the results are not always consistent with the aims.

Many of the differentiated uses discovered by SwiftKey may be conscious, revealing a sense of national pride paradoxically within a global environment. Cunliffe, Morris, and Prys (2013) found that young bilinguals (Welsh-English) on Facebook mixed their languages and that they used relevant words and symbols strategically to garner empathy for their perceived sense of ethnic individualism, which, of course, goes back considerably in time in that region. In other words, bilingualism and "mixed" or "collage" languages online are new strategies for asserting nationality and a new form of tribalism (Danet and Herring 2007). This implies a high degree of code switching among the languages and codes. Perhaps, as suggested previously, the emoji code is part of a global need to switch back and forth between the textual (purely language based) and the visual (open to a broader consensus of interpretation). It is relevant to note that National Public Radio (NPR) in the United States established a blog called "Code Switch" to examine the "frontiers of race, culture and ethnicity." The site points out that on a daily basis, young people confront the challenges and opportunities of code switching in digital spaces, at home and at school. The rules of the new communicative game in digital environments thus vary from one space to the next. Through mash-ups, cut scenes, YouTube, reality TV, and gaming, the code switching occurs not so much within a language as it occurs across media.

Today, one can custom-make emoji to suit culturally based preferences and then use them for specialized purposes. One website that allows for such self-styled construction is: http://www.myemojicreator.com/. Perhaps the emergence of all kinds of variable and specialized uses of the emoji code is a symptom of the need to retain and assert culture-specific identity in the context of global culture where individualism is fast becoming a thing of the past. On the other hand, as we have also seen, the use of emoji is certainly a conduit for establishing global modes of interaction based on a common ground of visual symbolism. The internet has, as McLuhan (1964) anticipated, generated a blend of individualism and tribalism in a "locked horns" way. This topic will be discussed in the final two chapters.

Cultural coding

Clearly, the question of cultural coding is a key one to understanding the functions and future use of emoji. The objective of the emoji code of providing a visual cross-cultural language is proving to be more difficult than was at first contemplated. The initial premise was based on the assumption that visually based symbolism is more free from ambiguity than language. But this is turning out to be a specious assumption. The culturally coded meanings assigned to common emoji and the usage contexts where they occur create a constant risk of ambiguity (Azuma and Ebner 2008). As Charles Peirce (1936–58) remarked throughout his writings, any sign or sign system is shaped by what he called the *interpretant*, which can be defined for the present purposes as the meanings that a sign evokes in some specific way; meaning is thus shaped by all kinds of contextualized forces, present and historical. The presence of the interpretant in the very nature of a sign entails the fact that further production of meanings arises as a sign is used. In Western culture, a cat is considered to be a domestic companion, among other things; in others it is viewed primarily as a sacred animal (akin to a sacred cow in some societies); and in others still it is considered to be a source of food (cat meat). Thus, while the emoji of a cat refers to virtually the same mammal in different cultures (no matter what specific form it takes), its interpretant varies considerably, constituting a source of supplementary (and obviously crucial) meanings.

As we saw with the poop emoji, the problem of ironic and humorous meaning is especially relevant in the process of cultural coding. Simply put, what is ironic or funny in one culture, may not be so in another and may even be offensive. The three emoji below, found in the text data constitute obvious amusing emoji to the Canadian students—the top one is a visual play on eggs (as delicious) being cooked in a pan—hence the caption of "eggcellent;" the middle one shows a computer screen that is alive and looks at the user, constituting a computer smiley of sorts with obvious satirical nuance; and the last one is a manga-style emoji conveying affection and fun through the pink eyeglasses, with the clenched "happy" fists, and the open mouth shouting out something happily:

Ironic-humorous emoji

Among the findings of the SwiftKey project (above) and other similar online statistical surveys, English-speaking nations are among the greatest users of emoji, and this might explain why many emoji are sorts of "visual jokes," given that humor in those nations seems to be a regular part of informal interactions via social media. The research team collected and examined various online social media texts in two other languages—Italian and Farsi—and found that the former used emoji sporadically in the same kind of informal messages and the latter even less so, despite adaptations of the emoji lexicon to specific cultural needs. In English-speaking nations, much more than in any other nation, it is now even assumed that emoji is the new slang of young people, as can be seen by public ad campaigns aimed at the adolescent demographic. Like PETA (previous chapters), the "Partnership for Drugs Free Kids" created an emoji-only campaign, in order to talk directly to teenagers and to stimulate debate about drug use and other topics of interest to adolescents, such as body image and bullying. The creators of the campaign asserted that the use of emoji also made it easier to discuss difficult topics that are hard otherwise to articulate meaningfully to the Millennial Generation in words only:

"Partnership for Drugs Free Kids" campaign

The message of this text can be reformulated in words as follows: "I'm tired of drinking or doing things to fit in (like an ant)." So, "I need to be strong and eat the right things and not to take drugs." Because the images are arranged conceptually (as discussed in Chapter 5), they allow the viewer to grasp the meanings directly without the intermediary of linguistic grammar. The text is indeed interpretable, as we found out with our informants, who easily read it and derived the underlying message from it instantly. They also proclaimed it to be highly effective. One informant put it as follows: "I know my younger brother would understand this much more than a prohibitive statement, which would sound like 'moralizing' to him. The message's tone is 'moralizing-free.'"

Such trends are begging a rather profound question: After millennia of attempts to impart literacy, reflection, and social improvement, along with the literary heritages that went with these attempts, are we throwing it all away in the service of friendly tone? Is "serious culture" a lost value? Or is emoji use simply an evolutionary outcome of hybrid writing? This very question will be discussed in the conclusion to this book.

Visuality

It is said, commonly, that today we live in a "visual culture," dominated by visual images emanating from all kinds of media outlets—cinema, television, comic books, websites, and so forth (Rampley 2005). For this reason, the term "visuality" has become a keyword for the study of emoji script, as suggested in previous chapters. The term "visuality" was coined by the Scottish historian Thomas Carlyle in his book *On Heroes* (1841), referring to the critical discourse of the "visualized heroism" of English imperial culture. In order for imperialism to be effective in garnering support it needs to be promulgated via visual images. Carlyle maintained that visuality, paradoxically, was also the antidote to imperialism, because of its unconscious persuasive effects. Thus, visuality was both a powerful expressive mode for promoting imperialism and a similarly powerful means for resisting it through reverse appropriation. The function of the emoji code is, arguably, compatible with this double sense of the word—it is both governed by forces of technological imperialism and, yet, it is subversive in the sense that it might potentially shatter the hegemonic writing practices of the Print Age.

One of the earliest critical studies of the power of visuality is the one by John Berger, *Ways of Seeing* (1972). Berger critiques how Western culture has used visual images ideologically, that is, to promote its capitalist agenda. The book itself is written in a hybrid script, consisting of seven chapters, four using words and images, and three only images, focusing particularly on how women are portrayed in advertisements and paintings generally. Since then, the study of visuality has burgeoned, overlapping with the psychological study of images and the use of images in the arts—a focus that ultimately comes from the influence of Rudolph Arnheim's key book, *Visual Thinking* (1969). In it, Arnheim challenged the traditional differentiation in philosophy and psychology between "thinking" versus "perceiving" and "intuition." He disputed the premise that verbal language comes before perception and that words are the triggers of thought. For Arnheim, perception and visual expression are what allow us to have a true understanding of our experiences of the world. In line with Arnheim's notion of visuality as a powerful means of knowing and communicating, it can be said that emoji literacy has ignited new ways of reading texts, which blends writing with visuality, and has thus brought about a largely unconscious visuality in thought and expression. This might explain why the emoji campaign above is effective with younger people, who have become accustomed to hybrid writing systems, whereas older ones are carrying over reading habits based on alphabetic script. So, age-based reading patterns are another source of variation in the interpretant applied to emoji texts.

Ekman (1985) also studied the relation between visuality and verbal language. He found a high degree of consistency across literate cultures in how they selected verbal labels that fit facial expressions such as those standing for happiness, sadness, anger, disgust, fear, and surprise. Ekman demonstrated that the same pattern extended to the preliterate Fore people in Papua New Guinea, whose members had not been exposed to media descriptions of expressive visual forms. Certain emotions, however, were accompanied with culture-specific prescriptions about who can show which emotions to whom and when. Ekman's research showed that universal features intersected with culture-specific ones in the naming of emotions (see also Bouissac 1999). As argued throughout this book, it is always difficult to sift out the universal from the specific, the general from the particular, perhaps because the brain is a blending organ that, like its expressive products, connects parts to the whole, as in symbols and other sign structures.

The emoji code may therefore reflect an inherent tendency of the human brain to think and express itself through visual percepts, as Arnheim maintained. Visual languages abound in modern-day society, from advertising to comics. It is relevant to note that Arnheim saw young people as naturally inclined to use visuality in order to come to grips with emerging questions about life, because these could be more easily envisaged in terms of artistic-aesthetic modes of expression, rather than words. Interestingly, there are various examples of contemporary literary writings that are similar to the emoji texts discussed in this book in form, if not in content. The Italian futurists, for example, combined images with text both to mirror the modern world and critique it at once. The difference between the futurist form of writing and the emoji form is a social one—futurism had an ideological objective, the emoji script has a mainly pragmatic one (to enhance aspects of communication). The goal of the futurists was to create a language free of syntax and prescribed rules of usage. Futurism was to writing what pop art was to visual aesthetics. Both attempted to bring the contemporary world into a new age of reading and understanding creative expression.

Emoji literacy certainly entails new forms of literacy and symbolism. As such, it is morphing into a symbolic, rather than purely iconic, language. This is perhaps why a specific emoji can elicit misinterpretation between users. It is assuming symbolic value more and more as it is used. At one level, therefore, the emoji code does indeed enhance communicability of common concepts across verbal languages, but at the interpretive level the transference effect comes into play. Moreover, since emoji grammar is based on conceptual structure, extracting meaning from an emoji text involves a high level of subjective interpretation.

Adjacency pair variation

Variation occurs not only at the level of cultural coding, but also in internal structural relations—a phenomenon that manifests itself especially in the variation shown in the construction of adjacency pairs. After interviewing the informants of the research group, we found in fact that outside of placement patterns at the end (closure) and at the beginning (salutation), the location of emoji within a text was seen as variable, reflecting the intentions of the sender to emphasize something. In other words, the placement was dictated by the sense of the word or words being used, with the emoji being placed, typically, right after them, to enhance meaning or add nuance to it. However, the choice of emoji was also governed by ease of selection. So, if the word "dog" came up, then the corresponding emoji was typically used to supplement the meaning, forming an adjacency pair, as mentioned in the previous chapter. The main reason for this was that the dog emoji is easily accessible on keyboards or in apps within a device. If, however, it was more arduous to look for an emoji to use in an adjacency pair, then most of the informants said they would skip the emoji usage, unless the message was very important to them, impelling them to look for an image on some online venue.

In themselves, the easily accessible emoji, chosen by Unicode, are intended to form a pictography of the everyday life of the users, etched into standardized images that everyone involved can easily understand, despite their potential symbolic nuances. This is why the most common ones, as we have seen, are used for salutation, punctuation, and general phatic and emotive functions. They have indeed become a core lexicon for standard emoji usage, since a smiley is more comprehensible across the globe as a form of salutation than is some language-specific formula. Some adjacency pairs also tend to have higher location on the universality scale, such as the word for "dog" and its accompanying emoji, just mentioned, although in such pairs cultural coding might surface unexpectedly. The emoji of a dog alongside the corresponding word generates an implicit self-contained cultural narrative about the role of dogs in the social milieu in which the users find themselves—dogs are pets, friendly, companions, and so on. In other cultures, this may not be the case, and thus the pair might be interpreted ironically, sardonically, or nonsensically.

Adjacency pairs are also subject to structural variation according to the flow of a conversation. For example, in the text of a previous chapter, which was a Christmas greeting one, the images used were all connected to Christmas—Santa Claus, tree, star, etc. This thematic consistency is typical of most of the messages investigated. But the way the text forced the viewer to locate the images in the textual structure also implied the focus that the sender wanted the receiver to grasp. Elsewhere, I have called this feature of textual structure "situational focusing" (Danesi 1994)—a use of discourse particles in order to get the interlocutor to focus on the sender's particular situation, thus highlighting it emotively. In going over the textual data collected for this book it became obvious that adjacency pairs allow the sender to emphasize some personal situation emotively according to their location. In the Christmas text, it was obvious that the sender was enthralled by the arrival of Christmas, since she was the "princess" in the family. And she seemingly wanted to bring her interlocutor into her subjective response to Christmas by showing him the situation it entailed visually.

Situational focusing implies that communication is an activity providing the expressive means for externalizing "ego-dynamic" states (Titone 1977). Interlocutors are engaged in bringing about the realization of personal agendas and goals through the emotivity of emoji. The interlocutors' affective responses to messages guide their choice of the images in the adjacency pairs. These are designed to take an addressee "into the situation" to which the addresser apparently wants to draw attention—it is a typical example of the conative function of communication. A simple example of situational focusing is the one above with the dog image accompanying the word for dog. In the context of the message the sender wanted to convey that his dog companion played a crucial role in his life, as the verbal text went on to imply—"He's my companion, wouldn't you wanna be as well?"—and thus to imply a romance of sorts. It is what Goodwin and Goodwin (1992: 181) have designated "assessments," that is, strategies which "provide participants with resources for displaying evaluations of events and people in ways that are relevant to larger projects that they are engaged in." In this fashion, the writer is able to provide a commentary either on his or her affective state, or on his or her perception of a situation.

The ego-dynamic function of emoji writing allows for a situational classification of adjacency pairs. So, in addition to highly emotive adjacency pairs, such as "I love u" followed by the heart emoji, the following categories can be used to refer to the ego-dynamic nature of such pairs:

1 *Annotation:* the emoji in a pair allows the sender to annotate his or her subjective response to something visually, as, for example, "this is awful" followed by the poop emoji.

2 *Sarcasm or irony:* the emoji in a pair is intended to be sarcastically critical of something, as in "I guess he's dating her after all" followed by the clapping emoji, 👏, as a sarcastic sign of "well done!"

3 *Wish fulfillment:* the emoji in a pair expresses a wish or desire on the part of the sender as in "finally, we're going out tonight" followed by a "let's boogie" emoji: 💃👯

4 *Synesthesia:* the emoji in a pair is intended to bring out the sender's state of mind through synesthesia, as in "I really luv her" followed by the fire emoji: 🔥

5 *Exhortation:* the emoji in a pair is meant to show exhortation. For example, the statement "I only wish this was true" was followed by a "divine exhortation" emoji, 🙏.

Although these ego-dynamic states can be elicited through words alone, it is much more effortful to do so. Moreover, the visual force of the images themselves guarantees that they are more easily communicable. The fact that there was considerable dissimilarity in the construction of adjacency pairs in the text data shows, overall, that internal variation is a constant factor in emoji usage.

Cartoon-style literacy

The discussion of variation brings us to a consideration of emoji writing itself, as a new form of literacy. In a way, writing an emoji text is tantamount to writing a cartoon strip. Adjacency pairs, for instance, are similar to cartoon images with a caption or a textual balloon. Moreover, like cartoons, the emoji code is typically intended to add humor, irony, friendliness, or other such emotive tinges to the text, thus enhancing its utterance functions. Emoji language could thus be easily classified under the rubric of "cartoon-style" writing, given especially its connection to pop-culture forms such as manga comics. Moreover, one can easily discern the three main social functions of cartoons in emoji usage:

1 *editorial cartoons*, which are created by newspaper or magazine artists in order to serve as commentary, usually of a satirical nature, on current events; this is identical to the annotative function of emoji described above;

2 *gag cartoons*, which are designed to usually ridicule or lampoon people and are found typically in magazines and on greeting cards; the use of satirical adjacency pairs abounds in the text data, constituting forms of "gags" meant to elicit laughter;

3 *illustrative* cartoons, which are found integrated with advertising or learning materials, serving to illuminate specific points or to bring out special aspects of a new product or educational topic; needless to say, the use of emoji to illustrate something in a message is common in all the text data examined for this book.

The cartoon-style writing inherent in the emoji code is undoubtedly associated with the advent and rise of cartoons as a modern hybrid form of narrative writing. And in the same way that cartoons are interpreted in vastly different ways across cultures (Cohn 2013), the cartoon style inherent in the use of emoji is a major source of culturally based variation. The tradition of cartoons, actually, started in the sixteenth century, with the German *broadsheets* (single cartoons printed on large pieces of paper), which were designed to sway people's opinions on some political or social issue. It was the English painter and engraver William Hogarth who initiated the art of pictorial (cartoon) storytelling—similar to the modern comic strip. In the subsequent nineteenth century, newspapers began including editorial cartoons in their publication format. In the United States, cartoonists like Thomas Nast used them to lobby for specific causes. Among his best-known works are cartoons about the American Civil War, and cartoons that inveighed against slavery. The gag cartoon was introduced by the *New Yorker* magazine in 1925. The practice of using poster cartoons began in the 1960s, when they started to appear usually as a vehicle for expressing political protest. The radical counterculture of the period produced a genre known as *underground comix*, which explored previously forbidden subjects (drugs, sexual freedom, and radical politics) in the form of cartoons. Today, online cartoons (known as e-toons) are used in all kinds of websites, with overlapping functions. The emoji code similarly offers the visual devices to inject satire and a form of editorializing into simple everyday messages.

With the advent of Twitter and Instagram, emoji writing, whether for cartoonish reasons or otherwise, has spread broadly, given that both provide useful apps for emoji selection, thus increasing the volume of emoji use (as mentioned above). Instagram is a video and photo sharing social networking service, enabling users to share visual images (pictures, videos, etc.) on other social networks, such as Facebook, Twitter, Tumblr, and Flickr. It would seem that texts created in these media almost always involve emoji, *de rigueur*. To ascertain this, we asked five informants if they could optionally not use emoji when communicating with friends via these platforms, for even one week, and all said unanimously that their texts would appear "weird" or "creepy" without the emoji. This indicates, albeit anecdotally, that emoji writing is no longer an option, but a matter of systemic writing style in certain contexts, platforms, and media. They are now part of a cartoon-style literacy that emphasizes humor and jocularity, rather than seriousness or reflective gravity.

Literacy practices are social practices. The two mirror each other. In a way, hybrid writing is (arguably) an unconscious social evolutionary reaction to the rigidity of linear phonetic writing and, especially, of the power relations that print literacy has entailed in the past—reflecting Carlyle's notion of visuality as a form of subversion against the status quo. According to some critics, such as Jacques Derrida (1976, 1978), print literacy practices have misguided us in answering existential questions by creating linguistic categories and precise definitions for this task, etching them into the vocabulary and grammar used to create texts. The assumption that language is a tool that encodes ideas without distortion is rendered useless when one looks at the history of writing and all the changes it has undergone. Derrida analyzed philosophical writings and found them to be highly entangled, circular, and serving the particular interests of the philosopher or the discursive ideology of the era in which a text was formulated. Writing, therefore, is hardly a tool for seeking truth, which is elusive by its very nature, but a means for encoding it in a specific way. The meaning of a written text cannot be determined in any absolute way because it shifts according to who reads it, when it is read, how it is read, and so on. Understanding a text is gained by reference to its individual parts and how these are collated into a whole. However, the parts cannot be understood without the whole, so the interpretation is circular. The meaning of the text must therefore be located or situated only in its cultural-historical context.

Derrida rejected the traditional way scholars interpreted literary works as reflecting the author's views. A narrative text has no unchanging, unified meaning, because the author's intentions cannot be easily determined. There are an infinite number of legitimate interpretations of a text that are beyond what the author intends. Hence, the text "deconstructs" itself over time. By their very nature, writing practices are self-referential. What appears to be the expression of truth in a text turns out to be only a specific opinion. Writing is thus a means by which cultural ideologies and "favored" opinions can be recorded for reproduction. What Derrida may have missed, however, is the fact that every form of expression reflects historical contextualization. This does not mean that it cannot be interpreted with different hermeneutics (modes of interpretation). With the addition of images to writing, hermeneutics has been overridden by poeticity, which is emotive, ego-dynamic, and resistant to rational logic in the philosophical sense—as an ordered presentation of facts. So emoji, like cartoons, have an anti-hegemonic subtext built into them.

Alphabets brought about the hermeneutic revolution in the ancient world, leading to the use of writing in place of orality as a means of recording information and of understanding the world rationally. This was so because, as McLuhan (1964: 9) observed, the alphabet "shapes and controls the scale and form of human association and action." McLuhan put forward four "laws" to which human artifacts (including writing) are purportedly subject: amplification, obsolescence, reversal, and retrieval.

These imply that a new invention or technology will at first amplify some sensory, intellectual, or biological faculty of the user; but, while one area is amplified, another is lessened or eventually rendered obsolescent, until the technology is used to maximum capacity and thus reverses its characteristics and a previous one is retrieved in another medium. As we have seen in this book, the hybrid emoji system of writing has indeed amplified the scope and reach of written informal communications, rendering parts of alphabetic practices obsolescent. But, today, print and other media of representation have been retrieved on the internet, which allows for reversals of all kinds, from print to purely symbolic textualities.

The social evolutionary aspects of hybrid cartoon-style writing need to be studied, of course, more empirically and neurologically, since visuality and verbality entail the engagement of different neural regions, as blending and other neuroscientific theories suggest (Chapter 4). This might mean a shift in cognition that both retrieves the past (pictography) and amplifies the present (hybridity). Cartoon-style writing is anti-hegemonic in the sense that it flies in the face of traditional literacy practices. Those who are literate—that is, those who can read and write—are those who have always wielded authority and influence throughout history. Before the late 1400s, the vast majority of people throughout the world were illiterate. Most had never had an opportunity to learn to read and write because there were few schools, and books were scarce and often expensive. Although some people at every level of society could read and write, most literate people belonged to the upper classes. Illiterate people relied on literate people to read and write for them. They were powerless and, to this day, illiteracy implies powerlessness and socioeconomic travail.

Literacy spread at an uneven rate until the invention of the printing press in the 1400s. Social class often determined who became literate. Literacy levels varied widely from region to region, even within one country. But the printing press changed all that. McLuhan characterized the new world shaped by the advent of the printing press, in fact, as the Gutenberg Galaxy, after the European inventor of the printing press, the German printer Johannes Gutenberg (as is widely known). Through books, newspapers, pamphlets, and posters, the printed word became, after the fifteenth century, the primary means for the propagation of information, knowledge, and ideas. More importantly, given the fact that books could cross political boundaries, the printing press set in motion the globalization of culture. It also encouraged the gaining of literacy across the world, paving the way for several paradigmatic movements, especially the Enlightenment.

With the spread of commerce and industry during the eighteenth and nineteenth centuries, large numbers of people migrated to cities where they were required to learn how to read instructions and perform tasks that required literacy. Governments began to value educated citizens, and systems of public schooling expanded. By the late 1800s, formal education had become common and mainly obligatory. As a result, more people had the opportunity and motivation to learn to read and write, causing the literacy rate to rise rapidly.

To this day literacy is considered to be the primary means for gaining social prestige and economic well-being. This is why many organizations work to improve literacy. But, as argued in this and previous chapters, literacy practices are changing. Although print literacy is still the norm in higher-register writing, from school and academia to journalism and philosophy, hybrid writing may soon creep into all levels of writing, recalling and retrieving (to use McLuhan's term again) the illuminated manuscript and rebus traditions of the past. The notion of critical literacy has now also become a target of acute interest, given the advent of hybrid writing. Critical literacy is the process of extracting meaning from print and putting meaning into print. This process is developed mainly through formal schooling, being reinforced by the social order in which literacy plays a dominant role. Critical literacy is shaped by the personality preferences of individuals and may develop further in later life. But there are also broader social functions of critical literacies that have shaped writing practices in the evolution of a society. There is, in other words, a power ideology behind them. Those with the highest levels of critical literacy tend to be power brokers with the ability to make themselves heard and noticed. Illiteracy generally assigns people to ghettoized communities. But the paradigm has shifted considerably. Cynthia Selfe (1999), for example, has argued that the notion of critical literacy has little relevance today unless it is related to computer and technological literacies, since the power alignments of the past have either dissipated or else migrated to online contexts, where they have been greatly modified. There is, in fact, a new form of anti-hegemonic literacy emerging in the Internet Age, and its most manifest symptom is in the use of hybrid writing.

Today, "looking up something" means either consulting a wiki or Google, rather than a print dictionary or encyclopedia. So, even the way we search for knowledge has changed drastically, let alone how we "write information" in texts. Online venues are thus becoming major sources of critical literacy and knowledge spread. The term *wiki* refers to any website that provides information of a specific kind—*Wikipedia* (encyclopedic), *Wiktionary* (dictionary), and so on. The difference between these and the traditional print sources (dictionaries and encyclopedias) is that they allow anyone to edit and change content, sometimes without the need for registration—a situation that obviously has implications for what literacy is.

The wiki phenomenon is not unrelated to the emoji one, since both are products of socio-evolutionary tendencies associated with digital technologies and the spread of a kind of global consciousness with respect to how knowledge is made and spread. Wikipedia was launched on January 15, 2002 by Larry Sanger and Ben Kovitz, who wanted, at first, to create an English-language encyclopedia project called Nupedia, to be written by expert contributors, in line with the internet-based encyclopedia project called the Interpedia (launched in 1993). But they soon made the decision to have it written and edited collaboratively by volunteers and visitors to the site. Needless to say, there has been controversy over Wikipedia's accuracy and overall reliability, since it is susceptible to the whims of users. The online encyclopedia has remedied this situation somewhat (especially with "warning" annotations), but it still remains a kind of marketplace reference source, where knowledge, like commercial products, can be negotiated, tailored, and discarded as the values of that marketplace change. The main idea behind Wikipedia is to bring the domain of knowledge and critical literacy within everyone's reach. The founders describe it as "an effort to create and distribute a multilingual free encyclopedia of the highest quality to every single person on the planet in his or her own language." It makes further research efficient by providing hyperlinks in each entry and other cross-referencing tools that facilitate the search for specific information. The articles are now also linked to other digital platforms. Wikipedia is thus not a rigidly created text, impervious to change without authoritative consent (as is the case in traditional encyclopedias). It allows anyone to be involved in knowledge construction in a continuing process of creation, reconstruction, and collaboration, thus ensuring that the knowledge source is constantly evolving and up to date. Critiques of Wikipedia are that it is inaccurate and poorly edited. This may be true, but the Wikipedians have started to turn it more and more into a traditional, quality-controlled online reference tool. Moreover, it seems that its infelicities soon get noticed and eliminated. Wikipedia is a self-organizing reference system. It has turned critical literacy into a populist rather than authoritative form of knowledge.

The same kind of argument can be made for emoji literacy. Access to emoji icons has turned the previous form of literacy into a more populist-based one, even though the emoji script is determined by institutions. It is the selection of the script in new creative ways of writing that constitutes the paradigm shift from the past. But one might ask if this is simply another case of power shifts, rather than of power attenuation. The shift from print-based literacy to digitally based forms is nowhere more evident than in the social power that Google itself has attained over a relatively short period of time. The company's declared goal is to organize information from around the world and make it accessible to anyone through the World Wide Web. The advent of Google has led to an intense debate about what constitutes critical or functional literacy. The noble idea of opening up all books and libraries to everyone via Google is highly idealistic, but it remains to be seen if it is practicable. There is now a new power paradigm. Knowledge is now in the hands of the digitizers, who will choose what to make available, even though Google has claimed that it will try to make "everything possible" available. There is great danger in giving one particular company, Google, enormous power. Another major issue with respect to the Google universe is the effects it might have on cognition, identity, socializing, and communication (among other things). Does Google make us more intelligent than in the past (since it purportedly entices more people to read) or more indifferent, making enormous amounts of information easily accessible but implicitly leading to its use without critical reflection? Suffice it to say that the reading and writing rules we use to understand the world contribute to shaping how we form our thoughts and how we perceive the world. And thus Google will unquestionably change our views of critical literacy and what it allows us to do cognitively. It is no coincidence that emoji are now available across the WWW for people to select, modify, and utilize in a *sui generis* fashion.

The greatest critique of emoji writing is that, like Google itself, it encourages ephemerality and an undue emphasis on "cartoonishness" (Auletta 2008; Carr 2008). Statistics and popularity rule the Google universe. Using algorithms, Google can easily determine the relevancy of sites and thus, by implication, assign value to the information available through measurement, rather than "intrinsic value" criteria. Rather than just ranking sites according to the number of times a particular search word is used, Google ranks them on the basis of the number of links the sites have. If a popular site is linked to a page, then that link is given even greater relevancy. Relevancy is thus tied to popularity. As Carr (2008) argues, Google has conditioned us to process information randomly, not in terms of systematic understanding. So, rather than encourage reading in the traditional Print Age sense of the word, Google is leading to selective and superficial browsing, guided by the criterion of popularity. As Vaidhyanathan (2011: 89) has put it, "We are not Google's customers: we are its product. We—our fancies, fetishes, predilections, and preferences—are what Google sells to advertisers."

Emoji writing certainly seems to fit in with this new "flow" of literacy practices established by the Internet Age. If one is to be a functional participant in this Age, then its emerging writing practices need to be evaluated for their utility and span of communicative possibilities. The emoji code has, in effect, become a lingua franca. Lingua francas have arisen throughout human history, often for commercial, scientific, or other official reasons. However, in the case of the emoji code, the reasons are limited to informal writing and, like cartoons, to enhancing the role of humor-based visuality in the construction of messages. And it is arguably this visuality that is a common source of variable usage and understanding of the emoji code across the internet.

Some warn of the dangers of this new kind of "superficial" lingua franca, since it may be endangering all languages, including English. But, as Susan Cook (2004) has argued, there is growing evidence that the new electronic landscape, unlike the real landscape, is not playing by the expected usual rules. This topic will concern us in the final chapter.

8 EMOJI SPREAD

Dear Internet: You are very good at spreading rumors. Truth is
more valuable and much harder to come by.

MARK FROST (B. 1953)

In 2015, Sony Pictures announced that it was planning on making a
feature-animated film based on emoji. Similar announcements were
made by other studios. Along with the Oxford Dictionary's choice of an
emoji for its Word of the Year, there were many signs that the use of emoji
had started to spread throughout society, at all levels. As we have seen
in previous chapters, emoji are now part of political campaigns, part of
logo-creation strategies for brands, and so on and so forth. They have
spread so broadly that, as we have also seen, they are now even used as
evidence in court trials, indicating that they are now intrinsic to human
interaction. Threats issued via emoji on platforms such as Facebook and
Instagram, are drastically changing the positive sentiments that emoji
are designed to evoke into a more sinister mode of communication.
Legal systems are now viewing menacing uses of emoji as constituting
harassment and even assault.

The spread of emoji throughout cyberspace is a phenomenon that has
profound implications for how the emoji code may evolve, not only in
semantic, grammatical, and pragmatic terms, but also in philosophical
terms. Why are emoji spreading throughout the digital landscape? What
does this imply for the future course of human writing and information
processing? These questions will be broached more concretely in
the next two chapters. Here, the objective is to look at the patterns of
emoji spread and how they may be changing in the very course of this
spread. Politicians, for instance, have jumped on the emoji bandwagon,
so to speak, en masse, turning political discourse more and more into a
cartoonish type of speech. Tweets from many politicians now invariably

contain emoji, perhaps to generate a positive tone to their messages and, by association, to the politicians themselves. The subtext to this type of usage seems to be: "How can you not like someone who is friendly and well meaning?" On the other side, people may want to react negatively (ironically) to politicians. Some websites, like the 2015 one created by the *Washington Post*, presents users with emoji of the American politicians involved in the presidential campaign that started in that year. It is reproduced here for the sake of illustration (http://tech.co/washington-post-political-emojis-2015-04):

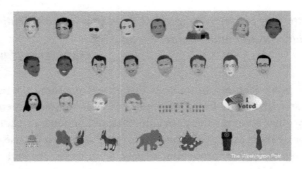

Political emoji

The images were used by voters in digital messages to react to the campaigners. In effect, the emoji code seems no longer limited to inter-friend communication contexts. It is spreading in ways that were likely unthinkable in 2010 when the code started being used throughout the world. This chapter will look at a few major trends in emoji usage as indicators of where the emoji movement may be heading (if anywhere). Specifically, it will examine the trend of writing only with emoji, the advent of emoji translations of written texts, and the use of emoji in advertising. The chapter concludes with a discussion of how effort guides the evolution of writing systems, including the emoji one.

Emoji-only writing

Hybrid emoji writing is, by and large, an amplification of traditional writing, adding emotive nuances to the text, and attenuating potential ambiguities of meaning or intent. As discussed, there are many precedents for this type of writing, from rebus forms to illuminated manuscripts.

Of course, there are other functions and aspects to the emoji phenomenon, as we have seen, but, by and large, emoji are meaning enhancers. In itself, this has few implications for the future of writing. However, writing texts completely in emoji is a completely different matter, since it is an attempt to penetrate writing practices radically and transform them completely. At present, this is not a widespread practice, but there are indications that it might be spreading.

In hybrid writing, emoji often clarify, illustrate, or reinforce a meaning, not obfuscate it. But in emoji-only texts, clarity of understanding is diminished considerably, as we have seen with the "birth story" text. These require understanding of both the conceptual and syntactic structure of the signs used, which are used to create texts much like collages.

Some texts are relatively easy to decode, using a basic rebus-processing approach, especially those that are translations of single and simple verbal phrases or expressions. The one below is well known in online venues; it translates the proverb "See no evil, hear no evil, speak no evil," followed by a pointing finger that, in some interpretations, can be translated as "leading the way" (i.e., it implies that the proverb should be followed):

Emoji translation of a proverb

However, what stands out here is that the emoji is a monkey—a choice that could create a polemical reaction, since the proverb is an ancient one with religious connotations. As far as can be determined, it has not created a stir, perhaps because it is consistent with the cartoonish nature of emoji literacy, giving it a kind of *sui generis* appeal to users of emoji who, presumably, have become accustomed to writing and reading in a cartoon-style mode. The research team searched, in fact, for critical reactions to this translation on the internet and was not able to find any significant ones that merit discussion here.

While this one was fairly easy to read, the following text—found on various websites—involves a moderate increase in the difficulty of decipherment. What aids in the interpretive process is the fact that the intent of the message is enunciated at the top in words—"Dude, let's rob a bank." This constitutes a guide to the decipherment of the emoji parts, which are arranged in list form, much like lines in a script or dialogue. They are the receiver's response to the exhortation to rob a bank in emoji form, thus clearly allowing the sender to visualize the consequences of such a suggestion. The top line portrays the sequence of events that are anticipated to occur in temporal order: gun (the weapon for robbing the bank) + money bag (the booty) + car (escape vehicle). This horizontal structure is episodic, mirroring the actual unfolding of events in sequential layout. The line below it is an emoji with grinning face and smiling eyes constituting an unsure and precarious reaction to the sequence above. The third line then paints what might happen next—police cars will be summoned to the scene. This is followed below by a frowning face—a logical reaction to the arrival of the police. The fourth line then portrays the likely scenario that will unfold after the police arrive: guns (shooting that will take place between the robbers and the police) + fire truck + ambulance (indicating the usual order of the arrival of these emergency vehicles, suggesting a possibility of injury). The final emoji is a double dizzy face, which is an expression of anxiety.

The final query from the sender—"So that's a no then?"—is the sender's conclusion that he draws from the emoji sequences. As can be seen, this message is decipherable because of the context provided by the verbal utterances, which provide an interpretative frame for decoding the emoji text. Without them, the message would become much more open to different interpretations. An example of such a text is the following one, also found on a public domain website:

The intent of the sender is clear—translating the television program *Doctor Who* into emoji. But the emoji-only assemblages are beyond comprehension to anyone not familiar with the program. The meaning of certain emoji can be inferred from the announced intent as, for example, the British flag (since the program is British), and the alien emoji (since the program is a science fiction one). But figuring out what the clocks and the other emoji stand for is virtually impossible without familiarity with the program. The emoji-only part leads the non-initiate interpreter into a blurry domain of blends and indirect references. As will be discussed below, a text of this type is resistant to global understanding, since it requires a high degree of inferential reasoning, rendering the reading process laborious. In sum, emoji-only writing is hardly a modality that is high on the universality scale; on the contrary, it seems to be highly specialized requiring specific kinds of knowledge, much like a jargon or technical language. Even the emoji translation of the proverb above requires the reader to be familiar with the proverb in the first place; without such background knowledge, it is unlikely that even that text can be read meaningfully.

Emoji translations

One of the more interesting trends in emoji-only writing can be seen in the fledgling attempts to translate alphabetic texts into emoji-only texts (as discussed briefly in previous chapters). In the area of the lyrics of pop songs, this has become a kind of trend. An example is the translation of Britney Spears's hit song *Toxic* (2003):

Emoji version of "Toxic" (2003)

The actual lyrics are widely known—"Baby, can't you see, I'm calling a guy like you should wear a warnin', it's dangerous, I'm falling, there's no escape. . ."—and need not be repeated here. However, without knowing them, decipherment would be difficult and produce a high level of variable readings. For example, one must either know, or figure out, that the pointing finger is a pronominal sign ("you"); also the use of the baby image for a paramour requires specific knowledge of the romance slang involved. We gave this text to several of the informants, who were children when the song came out and thus would not necessarily be familiar with it, asking them to translate it back into its lyrics. Overall, the subjects found it to be a fairly easy task, since they were familiar with the romance slang and, of course, with how to calque emoji onto words.

But, a number of the emoji were mistranslated or given a slightly different interpretation. Thus the text was not always reconstructed faithfully; it was approximated and inferred, even with the written word prompts.

Now, the decipherment of the above text is fairly straightforward and, even without knowing the original lyrics, can be reconstructed, as the informant group showed. But this is not always the case, and one wonders why, therefore, such translations are occurring with increasing frequency. One possibility is, as mentioned previously, that the emoji script, with its cartoon style, fits in perfectly with popular culture forms and trends. Thus, it should come as no surprise to find that pop artists, such as comedian Aziz Ansari, have become widely known users of emoji translations. Ansari translated the Jay-Z and Kanye West hit song, "Ni**as In Paris." This in itself became a pop trend, evidenced by the large number of clicks on Ansari's website. In response to this growing trend, there are now websites, such as Emojisaurus.com, which provide emoji translations of popular phrases.

The translation trend has penetrated all spheres of society, not only the pop-culture one. An example is Barack Obama's 2016 State of the Union address, which was translated by England's *The Guardian* with a Twitter account, @emojibama, constituting a transcript of his speech with a smattering of words. An excerpt is provided below:

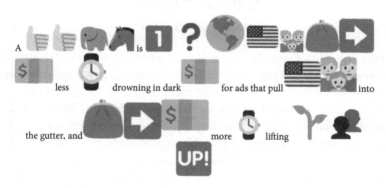

Emoji version of Obama's State of the Union speech

Though difficult to decode, it is certainly much more decipherable than, say, entire song lyrics, which require more specific knowledge. This translation helps guide the reading by adding words along with punctuation marks, giving the eye a break, so to speak, in the same way that a comma gives the traditional reading process a break. A survey of sites that reproduce important speeches or texts, however, shows that this is not yet a major trend. For the present, it remains a sporadic fad that is in sync with the cartoon-style effect that hybrid writing is generating and ensconcing.

The reading difficulty increases dramatically in the case of emoji translations of literary texts. One of the first books to be translated in this way is *Moby Dick*, by Fred Berenson, who published it as *Emoji Dick* in 2009. The first line of the novel is shown below. First, without knowing the line verbally, this sequence could be interpreted in a variety of other ways. Moreover, the emoji version lends itself to being perceived as a cartoonish updating of the text. As mentioned in the previous chapter, this might have anti-hegemonic overtones (vis-à-vis traditional literacy and literary forms). The use of a phone emoji for "call" is amusing because it is anachronistic—it renders the idea of "call," but it does so in a way that is dissonant with the era in which the text was written. The use of a sailboat and a funny whale emoji are also very cartoonish, giving the iconic first line of the novel a caricaturist feel, rendering it humorous and light, in contrast to the serious tone of that line in the novel.

Call me Ishmael.

First line of "Emoji Dick"

Even the title—*Emoji Dick*—seems to be a kind of joke. For traditional readers of *Moby Dick* this might be seen not as a light-hearted transcription, but a diminishment of the critical thought needed to understand the novel, thus trivializing it in a cartoonish way. On the other hand, it might produce interest in the novel through humorous devices that reach out to a new generation of potential readers, accustomed to emoji style.

Berenson has also established an "Emoji Translation Project" for creating an engine that can be used to translate all kinds of books. There might be ways of truly translating verbal texts into emoji ones with no loss of the seriousness content, but in my view this may never be totally realizable given the nature of the emoji code. Another emoji translation project worth discussing here is the one of Lewis Carroll's *Alice in Wonderland* by designer and author Joe Hale (2015). Hale starts with an emoji syntagm: backhand pointing down + rabbit + heavy large circle emoji, to indicate Alice's journey down the rabbit hole. Alice is represented throughout by the princess emoji, the Cheshire cat as a smiling cat face with open mouth, the Mad Hatter with a top hat emoji—so that each emoji character is as close as possible to the description of the Carrollian character. Over 25,000 separate emoji were used, and the entire text looks like this:

Emoji translation of "Alice in Wonderland"

What immediately catches the eye here (no pun intended) is that the density of the text makes it virtually impossible to read it without the verbal version at hand for consultation. The effort to decipher the text is truly gargantuan, having a very high level of what has been called in this book visual noise. Hale himself has answered this issue rather cleverly on his website, pointing out that Carroll's work is a narrative treatise on the human imagination, and thus that his translation is "a visual aid to inspire the imagination and think about the magical world of Wonderland." This is certainly an admirable goal, but it still boggles the mind as to how one can "read" such a text, let alone use the imagination to enter into its conceptual complexity. Unlike *Emoji Dick,* though, this translation may be more in sync with the readership, since the novel was intended mainly for children. Hale has also translated J. M. Barrie's *Peter Pan*, calling it *Neverland*. He claims that his inspiration came, in part, from Jung's archetype theory, which claims that primordial images are part of the collective unconscious of humanity, finding expression in various symbolic forms. It is hard to discern, however, where the archetypal forms are in the above text. When we presented the text to the informants in the research group, there were two reactions. First, everyone was flabbergasted by the visual complexity of the text, saying that it would take "too much time and effort" to figure it out. Second, and more significantly, several mentioned that it seemed to be a trivialization of the novel which they enjoyed as children, reading it, incidentally, mainly in illustrated books with accompanying pictures to illustrate, not replace, the words.

In sum, it stands to be seen if translations of this type will spread and become common. Given the effort needed to decode them, and the inability of the emoji code to penetrate serious content, my own sense is that they will not gain popularity.

Emoji in advertising

Perhaps in no other domain is the spread of emoji so powerful and effective as in the advertising one. Below is the emoji ad of Domino's pizza that the company uses on its Twitter site (at the time of writing this book) to promote its "Order Pizza Via Twitter" service:

Domino's pizza ad

Deciphering the ad is relatively easy, since its main visual focus is on the pizza slice and how the different slices can be arranged to be eaten. A verbal counterpart might be: "Hungry for a slice of pizza? Have one or more of our slices!" or something similar. Actually, the fact that many verbal paraphrases are possible indicates how a visual code generates meaning through what has been called here the thesaurus effect. In a verbal slogan, only one of the paraphrases would be required; in a visual slogan, many more paraphrases are implied.

This kind of advertising is showing up throughout the brand world. McDonald's has even transformed emoji forms into characters, as can be seen in one of their ads below:

McDonald's emoji ad

The conceptual metaphor involved here is rather transparent—people are emoji. The McDonald's campaign is named, in fact, "Everyone is an Emoji." Is this a simple attempt to appeal to millennials who have been reared in a world of mobile devices, text messages, and social media? Is it an attempt to tap into that generation's desire for constant friendly contact and thus eternal sunshine?

Again we asked the members of the research group who were born in the mid- to late 1990s, and thus could be construed as millennials, to evaluate the McDonald's campaign, which took place primarily in Europe and especially in France. Virtually all pointed out that it "was a joke." Many even interpreted it ironically and critically, seeing it as a ploy to attract them unnecessarily. While a few saw the ad as "disturbing," they hastened to add that other trends in advertising were similarly disturbing. Actually, two of the informants directed the research team to a subvertisement of this ad campaign created by HuffPost UK Comedy on its website—a subvertisement is an ad that satirizes or critiques a real ad or ad campaign:

good times.

Emoji subvertisement

In some cases, however, it is difficult to see how an emoji-only ad can benefit the company involved. Consider the ad below by Chevrolet to promote its 2016 Chevy Cruze which is, clearly, difficult to decipher:

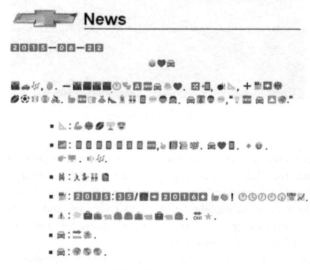

Chevrolet emoji ad

We asked the informants in the research group to translate the ad into words. Some had already seen it, but virtually all of them expressed difficulty in translating it. However, a few said that maybe the whole point of the ad is to get a whole sense of the car, "viewing" the experiences to which it is associated from top to bottom (to drive children around, to put bags in it for travel, and so on). The visual text suggests, not describes.

The ad below for Bud Light is another example of how the suggestiveness of emoji can be used advantageously. It has reconstructed the American flag to celebrate the Fourth of July holiday with fireworks emoji in place of the "stars," and beer glasses with flags in place of the "stripes."

Bud Light emoji ad

The ad is transparently evocative of Andy Warhol's serial silkscreen painting technique, where an object, such as a flag, would be reproduced over and over to mirror the assembly-line manufacturing process that produced it. Indeed, many of these ads are imitative of pop art, with its pastiche style. The marketing world has even expanded the emoji code on its own, to get around the limitations imposed by the preset Unicode system. There are now custom-branded emoji keyboards and sticker campaigns allowing brands to reach their consumers much more individualistically. Interestingly, Warhol was a designer of shoe ads before venturing into the domain of pop art, allowing him to grasp the cultural meanings of commercial products and to express them subsequently in paintings. The pop-art movement was inspired by the mass production and consumption of objects. But despite its apparent absurdity, many people loved pop art, no matter how controversial or crass it appeared to be. The emoji ads come on the coattails of this mind-set. Some artists duplicated beer bottles, soup cans, comic strips, road signs, and similar objects in paintings, collages, and sculptures; others simply incorporated the objects themselves into their works. As Hoffman (2002: 101) has aptly put it:

> Pop art, like advertising, is interested in the concept more than the rendering. It uses the objects that inhabit the world every individual

of every class takes for granted—the mundane, mass-produced stuff that is all around us. The things you use and like. Pop artists don't use these things because there is nothing else to paint, they use them to make a point.

Already in 1913, the French-American artist Marcel Duchamp produced an upside-down but otherwise unaltered Bicycle Wheel, asserting that it (or any other everyday object) constituted a sculpture if an artist declared it to be so. Duchamp soon followed the work with a bottle rack, snow shovel, and most notoriously, a urinal. The attitude of Duchamp and other members of the so-called Dada movement who shared his views about art reemerged in the early 1960s through an international group of artists calling themselves Fluxus. Like the Dadaists, they sought to erode the barriers between art and life and allow randomness and chance to guide their work. The Dada movement led to the pop-art movement which, in turn, brought consumer objects into the realm of art. The emoji ads certainly fall into this pop-art-culture flow, blending different artistic media into a pastiche of meanings.

The McDonald's ad above is clearly a Dadaesque work, with absurdity built into it and at the same time evocative of the absurdist times in which we live, as the informants pointed out. The Pepsi Twitter ad is another example of pop-art cartoonish style. The message consists of the emoji slogan syntagm: cool + thirsty = Pepsi + happiness:

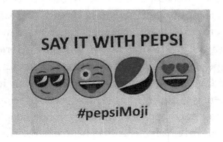

Pepsi emoji ad

Effort

The discussion in this chapter leads to considering an inherent principle of human communication—writing systems tend to evolve toward the diminution of the effort required to create and understand texts. If emoji-only texts are effortful to read, then the reverse principle is implied—namely that this type of writing will not survive. Even a cursory look at older versions of a language will illustrate that the effort-saving principle is operative in all communicative codes. All one has to do is read a page from Chaucer or even Shakespeare to realize that English writing involved much more effort to understand.

French linguist André Martinet (1955) argued that languages in general evolved over time to make communication more economical so as to preserve effort. Reviving a notion articulated by William Dwight Whitney in 1877, Martinet posited that complex language forms and structures tended toward reduction. This principle was further elaborated by the French scholar Guillaume Ferrero in 1894, discussing it in an article that laid out previously undetected facts about reductive phenomena in language evolution. Benoit Mandelbrot (1954, 1983), who developed fractal geometry, became fascinated by the implications of this principle, detecting in it a version of what is called a "scaling" law in biology.

Now, emoji writing can certainly be seen to increase the economy of writing, since each emoji can stand for many nuances that would otherwise have to be articulated in phrases and even sentences (the thesaurus effect). And, of course, they make reading texts much less effortful, since they literally "show" meanings holistically. But emoji-only texts such as the translations above, seem to go contrary to the principle, requiring significant effort to read. It is perhaps for this reason that such writing will likely not spread. We asked the informants of the research group if they thought that emoji novels such as the *Emoji Dick* one would become popular. All of them answered in the negative. Most said that they could not replace the serious meanings of words in elaborate texts, although a number of them, who were native Chinese speakers, pointed out that visual languages can express all that alphabetic ones can and more. A few also mentioned that diagrams and charts are really similar to emoji in how they allow, for instance, mathematicians and scientists to compress a lot of information into visual form. This sophisticated answer came, of course, from university students, but it is now reflective of how everyone perceives the writing of information on websites, which also might contain graphic elements (tables, charts, etc.).

The informants remarked that reading texts such as the *Emoji Dick* and *Alice in Wonderland* ones is bizarre, since it would constitute too much effort to do so. They also pointed out that it is unlikely that they would ever write in this way, not only because it would take significant effort, but also because no one would take the time to read their messages. One student pointed out that: "It is efficient to use emoji, because it takes so little effort to do so." In other words, short messages seem tailor-made for emoji use, since in this case the emoji code does not entail an increase in effort, but, instead, a more economical and effective way of conveying tone and nuance. So, in line with the least effort principle, it would seem that hybrid emoji writing might persevere and spread even more in the future. Its objective of maintaining a positive sentiment is what makes it a useful code. The informants provided the following relevant insights on this question:

1 "Yeah, I use emoji, to keep my friends, friendly, you know?"

2 "I like to make my texts funny or just fun."

3 "When I'm angry at my friends, I always add emojis to make them smile."

4 "After we fight, I send him a text with many emoji to show him I still love him."

5 "I automatically start and end with smileys because I wanna make sure my friend always likes me, no matter what I have to tell her."

6 "I don't know. I just like to use them. So, instead of using 'lol' or 'see u', as I used to do, I now use emoji; they talk to my friends much more."

7 "I love the faces; they're better than the 'lol' or 'love u' I used to use; that's so passé."

8 "Yeah, they're fun; better than 'lol' and much more friendly."

The last three statements are especially insightful, since they suggest that the type of abbreviated writing that had emerged in digital writing may have been a passing trend. The term *netlingo* was coined by David Crystal (2006) to describe this type of writing, with its compact forms such as: "How r u?" = "How are you?"; "g2g" = "Got to go," and so on. The forms increase efficiency while reducing physical effort since time is saved in the hand actions performed on keyboards. Crystal (2006: 87) called this the "save-a-keystroke principle." Most of netlingo is thus not case-sensitive, involving the random use of capitals or no capitals at all. Abbreviated writing was used by the Greeks as early as the fourth century BCE, gradually evolving into a true shorthand code, known as *tachygraphy*. The Roman slave Tyro also developed shorthand writing around 60 BCE, apparently for recording the speeches of Cicero. Scholars and scientists have always used abbreviations of various kinds to facilitate technical communications among themselves, making them precise (*etc., et al., op. cit. N.B.*). In this case, abbreviation implies a high level of specialized literacy. Also, we abbreviate the names of friends and family members (*Alex* for *Alexander*), common phrases (*TGIF* for *Thank God it's Friday*), and anything else that refers to something or someone familiar.

But what sets the abbreviation tendencies in netlingo apart from the past is the speed and extent to which they are spreading and becoming part of communicative behavior throughout the internet and also migrating to the offline world. There is an expectation in the internet universe that responses to emails, text messages, and the like must be rapid, whether the medium is synchronous or asynchronous. Logically, abbreviation helps people meet this expectation by making it possible to "get back" to the sender more quickly. It is in this communicative environment that the emoji code has emerged, often replacing the abbreviated forms of netlingo. Given that emoji are available on keyboards, they too reflect the save-a-keystroke principle even more so, since in text abbreviations several keystrokes are still needed; in emoji only one stroke is needed to select the specific emoji required.

9 UNIVERSAL LANGUAGES

If particulars are to have meaning, there must be universals.
PLATO (C. 429–C. 347 BCE)

The spread of the "light-hearted" emoji code further and further into the social landscape forces one to take it more seriously—no ironic pun intended. Initially, the makers of the code had a rather noble motivation—to facilitate communication among the denizens of the global village independent of their language or culture. The premise for doing so—the universality of visuality—was, and still is, a legitimate one, since, as the history of writing saliently demonstrates, picture writing is ancient and, arguably, more comprehensible across time and cultures than are alphabetic forms of writing. But this goal, while admirable, has hardly been achieved and, indeed, the emoji code has found a specific communicative niche in the digital universe as a code for establishing and maintaining amicability in tone in informal texts. Its spread to other domains, such as the advertising and political ones, is strategic, rather than evolutionary. Advertisers, politicians, pop musicians, and the like see the emoji code as an opportunity to establish contact with specific audiences so as to portray themselves as friendly, trustworthy, and *au courant*. If the emoji code is ever to become a true universal language, it cannot become fractured through usage or become too diversified through cultural coding.

Despite the variation that has entered the emoji code (discussed in previous chapters), it certainly has implications for what a universal form of language might look like, if one were possible to construct in the first place. Above all else, such a language would likely have picture-words like emoji. Moreover, it should facilitate ease of reading, not inhibit it. This suggests that hybrid writing is more likely to be located high on the universality scale and thus remain, while emoji-only writing, as we saw, is unlikely to spread because it requires too much effort on the part of the reader and will thus fall on a lower level on the scale.

Overall, it is obvious that the emergence of the emoji movement has definite implications in the context of the globalization of communications. Unlike other universal language movements, such as the Esperanto one, the emoji phenomenon springs from a desire to enhance the reach of communication among users of different languages, without replacing them; for this reason, it has had a broader reach than other artificial languages, since it does not radically threaten the survival of linguistic diversity, as we have seen throughout this book, nor does it require learning the new universal system like a foreign language. No special training is needed to learn emoji use. But will this experiment in picture writing last? As systems of communication evolve, and rapidly so in the digital age, perhaps the emoji code is just another fad, as hinted at previously, tapping into a comic book or cartoonish mind-set that is characteristic of pop-culture style in all domains of human interaction. On the other hand, it does seem to signal an ever-broadening hybridity in representation that comes from living in the digital age. As an informal code, it might indeed spread further and institutionalize itself in the future. The latter issue will be discussed in the next chapter. The objective of this one is to consider the nature of universal language experiments of the past and how the emoji movement fits in with these.

Artificial languages

Because language mirrors social conditions, including inequities, and because speaking a different language is perceived broadly by people across the globe as instilling a sense of difference between "Us" and "Them," and thus a potential source of misunderstanding and conflict, many have dreamed of creating an artificial, universal language, which all people could speak and understand unambiguously and which would not encode any inequalities acquired by different languages through the channels of history and culture-specific traditions. The rationale given for constructing such a language is thus a rather laudatory one—if all people spoke the same tongue, misunderstanding among cultures could be reduced, cultural and economic ties might become much tighter and less conflictual, and good will would increase between countries and between people.

None other than René Descartes is believed to have originated the idea of a universal or common language in the 1600s, although the quest for a "perfect language" goes back to the Tower of Babel story, in which God punishes humanity for its hubris of wanting to build a structure reaching heaven. His punishment was giving humans multiple languages, so that they could not understand each other and thus fail in their attempt to build the tower. Incredibly, more than 200 artificial languages have been invented since Descartes put forth his proposal. The seventeenth-century clergyman, John Wilkins, wrote an essay in which he proposed that a true universal language would have words in it that were free of ambiguity. *Volapük*—invented by Johann Martin Schleyer, a German priest, in 1879—was one of the earliest attempts to construct such a language that would gain moderate diffusion. The name of the language comes from two of its words meaning "world" and "speak."

Today, only Esperanto is used somewhat as an artificial language. As is well known, it was devised by Ludwik Lejzer Zamenhof, a Polish physician. The name of the language is derived from the pen name he used, Dr. Esperanto, on the book he published describing it, *Fundamento de Esperanto: Lingvo Internacia* (1887). The word means, as Zamenhof explained it, "one who hopes." Esperanto has a simple, uniform structure—for example, adjectives end in /-a/, adverbs end in /-e/, nouns end in /-o/, /-n/ is added at the end of a noun used as an object, and plural forms end in /-j/. Its core vocabulary consists mainly of root morphemes common to the Indo-European languages. The following sentence is written in Esperanto: *La astronauto, per speciala instrumento, fotografas la lunon* = "The astronaut, with a special instrument, photographs the moon." As can be seen, the fact that its structure and vocabulary is based on Indo-European languages already limits its universality, especially among speakers of non-Indo-European languages. Its closeness to Romance languages, such as Spanish, would make it easily understandable to speakers of those languages; but this constitutes an obvious bias toward such languages, thus decreasing its universality.

Esperanto was also designed to obviate fracturing of any sort and, as described by Zamenhof, to be immune from outside interferences that would introduce variation into its grammar and vocabulary. However, research on Esperanto has shown that it is, ironically, undergoing changes, due to external interferences caused by simple usage. Benjamin Bergen (2001), for instance, discovered that even in the first generation of Esperanto speakers, the grammatical structure of the language had, apparently, undergone simplification and diversification. The details need not concern us here. The point is that Esperanto has mutated through usage. Some estimates peg the number of speakers of Esperanto from 100,000 to over a million. It is difficult to accurately determine the number, because there is no specific territory or nation that uses the language exclusively. Zamenhof actually did not want Esperanto to replace native languages; he intended it as a universal *second* language, providing a new lingua franca for communication among people of different linguistic backgrounds. Today, Esperanto continues to have speakers (or more correctly followers). The Universala Esperanto-Asocio (Universal Esperanto Association), founded in 1908, has chapters in almost 120 countries. Cuba has radio broadcasts in Esperanto. There are a number of periodicals published in Esperanto, including *Monato*, a news magazine initially printed in Belgium. Some novelists, such as the Hungarian Julio Baghy and the Frenchman Raymond Schwartz, have written works in Esperanto. There is no evidence, however, that Esperanto has surfaced in digital communications as a lingua franca of sorts.

In medieval Europe, Latin had been raised to the level of a common language for specific literacy purposes, and thus for centuries it was used by theologians, scholars, and scientists to communicate among themselves across Europe. A little later French took its place, hence the term *lingua franca*. Today, English is the lingua franca (and should thus be called more accurately *lingua anglica*), given its prevalence in all kinds of cross-cultural communicative settings.

There are also constructed languages that are intended to serve artistic or narrative purposes, rather than universal communication. These are the languages made up by writers, such as Quenya and Sindarin, found in J. R. Tolkein's *The Lord of the Rings* series of books, and Klingon in the *Star Trek* series of television programs and movies. These are interesting because they show, above all else, that artificial languages can be easily constructed in the same style (grammatical and lexical) as natural languages. So, whether specific languages arise historically, or whether they are constructed for specialized purposes, all languages will reflect the same kinds of structures. Sometimes, an artificially constructed language is designed to point out gaps in a natural language. Lewis Carroll, as is well known, invented his own artificial language, in his poem *Jabberwocky*, to show that the English language as constituted does not tell all there is to tell about reality. He coined words such as the following to fill gaps that he argued needed to be filled. Note that they have the phonetic and grammatical structure of English words just the same: *brillig* = the time of broiling dinner, that is the close of the afternoon, *slithy* = smooth and active, *tove* = a species of badger with smooth white hair, long hind legs, and short horns like a stag, *wabe* = side of a hill.

There are also many artificial computer languages, such as Interlingua, used in the making of computer algorithms, which need not concern us here, since these have a specific usage. They are interesting in themselves, since they attempt to model human languages stripped down to their structural core, with the premise being that this core is the blueprint for human language. This whole line of argument, though, would take us away from the present purposes (see Danesi 2016).

Unlike Esperanto, and similar languages, the emoji code is made up of picture-words that stand for a variety of concepts that could, actually, be expressed with the existing lexical categories of a language, as we have seen. But is it truly a means toward developing a universal visual or symbolic language? Before answering this question, it is relevant to briefly revisit Leibniz's *characteristica universalis* as a framework for formulating an answer. Leibniz's term is translated, appropriately, "universal character." He believed that a system of visual universal characters could be developed to express common philosophical, mathematical, and scientific concepts unambiguously. His goal was, therefore, to make technical communications easier and free of misunderstanding. His basic construction technique was ideographic, based on Chinese characters, at least as understood by Europeans in Leibniz's era. The global expansion of economic, scientific, and political relations in that era made his project, actually, a more broadly practical one, prefiguring the modern Internet Age, even though Leibniz critiqued attempts to create universal languages, such as the one by Wilkins (mentioned above), for everyday practical purposes. He maintained that his system was to make mathematical and scientific concepts much more precise, free of the vagaries of language.

Of particular interest to the present discussion is the fact that Leibniz wanted to make his signs more "natural" rather than "conventional." He illustrated his idea of what a natural sign was with diagrams, such as the ones on the frontispiece of his *De Arte Combinatoria*, each of which was meant to stand for Aristotle's notion that all things are formed from a combination of the basic elements—earth, water, air, and fire. As can be seen, these are hybrid forms, made up of the word and its pictorial representation:

Leibniz's pictograms

As Cohen (1954) has cogently argued, Leibniz's language is based on three main criteria that can easily be employed to define what a code would require in order to become a universal one. These are as follows:

1 It would have to function as an "international auxiliary language," allowing people of different linguistic backgrounds to communicate with each other.

2 It would have to create a symbolism that could easily accommodate future knowledge.

3 It would have to be an instrument of demonstration of basic concepts.

Mapping the emoji code against each of these criteria suggests that it has the potential to evolve into a universal code. It certainly is an auxiliary language, since it can be easily incorporated into the texts written in any system. But, unlike the *characteristica*, it is a specific kind of auxiliary language—it is used primarily in short informal communications. As for the second criterion, emoji can be modified, amplified, and constructed in many ways to accommodate future needs, even though in this case the modifications fragment the code, thus weakening its potential universality. And, needless to say, it certainly is in line with the third criterion—a fact that needs no commentary here.

Blissymbolics

Perhaps the only true *characteristica universalis* project to have had any significant impact in international communications is the one by Charles Bliss (see 1949, 1955, 1978, 1985) and his semantographic movement. It is reported that, while living in China, Bliss became interested in Chinese shop signs, which he erroneously thought were written in ideographic script. He learned how to read them, with back-up training, eventually coming to the realization that he had been reading them not in Chinese, but through the conceptual filter of his own language of German. From this experience, he set out to develop a system of picture writing recalling Leibniz's system, attempting to make written communication universal through the construction of symbols that could be easily comprehended by anyone.

The system he developed, called Blissymbolics, caught the attention of psychologists and educators, because it produced genuine results. In 1965, a teaching center in Canada adopted Bliss's system successfully to teach children with cerebral palsy to read and write. Bliss himself saw this as a use of his system for the wrong reasons. He criticized the center acerbically, but eventually his symbols were incorporated fruitfully into various therapeutic-clinical pedagogies designed for children with learning problems. Despite Bliss's objections, this usage brought his system of writing to the forefront as a pedagogically effective one.

The Blissymbolic script now consists of over 2,000 symbols which can be combined together to create an infinite variety of new symbols and expressive structures. The comparison between these symbols and emoji shows many analogies and isomorphisms, but also fundamental differences. The main one is that the Bliss system was devised with a particular goal in mind—to make one writing script available throughout the world; that is, he wanted his system to replace existing writing systems. Emoji were devised instead not to replace these systems, but to spruce them up visually so as to make digital communications more understandable among speakers of different languages. Moreover, given the changes that have been occurring in emoji usage, it is becoming more and more a kind of "epigenetic language"—that is, a language that is shaped by users and uses. Blissymbolics is impervious to external pressures of change.

Bliss's system was devised in an era of expanding international tourism and communications. This led many to believe that a new symbol-based language was needed to facilitate global interactions. Blissymbolics, to some, was the perfect solution. In theory, Blissymbolics would be free from epigenetic interferences. He saw the path to developing his system while he was in Shanghai, becoming entranced by Chinese characters, which he could largely figure out for himself. He hired an instructor so that he could both confirm his own decipherments and learn more about Chinese writing. Of particular importance was his discovery that a written text could be read by a Chinese person no matter what his or her particular native language or dialect was. He also realized that his own reading of the texts was in terms of German or English. He thus concluded that a universal script based on picture signs could be envisaged for international communications, which would allow for the transcription of any language, thus providing a universal symbol code for writing tasks of all kinds. In the quest to develop a system of pictorial writing, based on his belief that such writing would achieve the final victory over phonetic scripts, Bliss started work on his system in the early 1940s.

Blissymbolics turned out to be similar to Leibniz' *characteristica*, consisting of a set of small figures or picture symbols in place of written words for them that would have the capacity to stand for visible objects and ideas in outline form, as in geometry and other mathematical diagrammatic practices. The assumption in all these systems was, however, that there is a universal structure to semantics, but a differential one in the ways that it is expressed. Synchronizing the two—via a common symbolic script—would lead to a truly universal language, hence Bliss's term "semantography," which alludes to this very fact. The long title of his first book on his system essentially encapsulates this intention:

International Semantography: A Non-Alphabetical Symbol Writing Readable in All Languages. A Practical Tool for General International Communication, Especially in Science, Industry, Commerce, Traffic, etc. and for Semantical Education, Based on the Principles of Ideographic Writing and Chemical Symbolism.

Bliss claimed in the book that his symbols were meant to be readable by anyone, no matter what language he or she spoke. Not surprisingly, his system was instantly applauded by mathematicians and logicians, such as Bertrand Russell, who themselves sought to develop logical sign systems that could be applied to the representation of semantic notions in a universal fashion. Bliss endorsed this view at first, but as the world changed with an explosion of tourism in the late 1950s and early 1960s, he modified it somewhat. As reflected in subsequent editions of his book, he realized that picture symbols could provide a broader semantic bridge among users of different languages, not a perfect one. Apart from logicians, however, many resisted Bliss's system. The fact that it was used successfully to teach children with cerebral palsy to read and write phonetically was a source of vindication for Bliss, despite his initial objections. He hoped that eventually his system would spread and be used at schools across the world to teach all kinds of children. But like the Montessori method, it attracted only a particular type of teacher who wanted to step outside the traditional molds of the classroom and to adopt a seemingly more effective method of teaching literacy. For this reason, it never really spread throughout education, being constrained to special situations. Overall, it is estimated that Blissymbolics are used today in more than thirty countries.

Presently, there are a couple thousand semantographic symbols, made up of basic shapes that are easy to write and which can be combined to compose new symbols ad infinitum. They can also be used to write sentences in any language. Below are some basic symbols:

Compound symbols

love	tool	conscience	car, vehicle	bus	aeroplane	camera	garden

Words

friend	pet	happiness	like	dislike	education	teacher	school

theatre	library	hospital	post office	city	village	telephone	office

Examples of Blissymbolics

It is absolutely interesting to note that some of these are similar to emoji, such as the use of the heart symbol to convey love and happiness and the basic shape of a house as the symbol for habitations of various kinds. Bliss classified his symbols into three general categories—material things, energy (actions and activities), and human values. In natural languages these would be realized grammatically as substantives, verbs, and adjectives. In Blissymbolics the grammatical functions are marked by specific symbols—a square, a cone, and an inverted cone, which are placed above a semantic symbol in order to identify it as a thing, action, or value. Bliss claimed that these symbols mirrored human perception, whereby, for example, the square symbol indicated that the structure of matter is systematic, not random. Needless to say, no such markers exist in emoji, which is a semantic script, achieving grammatical structure through placement, as we have seen.

Bliss designed his symbols to be both pictographic, for those concepts that could be represented easily through visual resemblance, and ideographic, to represent more abstract concepts. Also, the dimensions and orientations of the symbols modify their meanings. Many of these function like morphemes in language—particles such as affixes that modify the meaning. Putting these together then allows for the easy construction of sentences. The sequence below corresponds to the English sentence "I want to go to the movies":

Blissymbolic sentence

The pronoun "I" is constructed with the character for person (an upright stick on a platform) and the number "1" (standing for "first person"). The number "2" would thus stand for "you," and so on. The heart symbol stands for desire or wanting, while the serpentine symbol ("fire") emphasizes this meaning. The inverted cone figure on top identifies the symbol as a verb. The third figure stands for "to go" and is composed of the Blissymbol for "leg" and, of course, the cone symbol for verb. The last symbol, which stands for "movies" is constructed with the house figure followed by the film character ("camera") with the arrow indicating movement.

Comparing this syntagm with the emoji ones of the last chapter will show that it is much more marked for comprehension, once the symbolism is learned, whereas in emoji-constructed texts, comprehension is embedded in the hybridity of the text, as we have seen.

It is relevant to note that a proposal was made around 2009 to include Blissymbolics into the Universal Character Set for use in the iSO/IEC 10,646 and Unicode Standard. However, the proposal never came to fruition, for various reasons that need not concern us here. Suffice it to say that Blissymbolics has so far not made it to digital platforms that would allow it, like the emoji code, to spread broadly across the world. One reason that may inhibit this, in addition to the technical ones, is that Blissymbolics is a substitutive script that would eliminate all scripts. This goal raises obvious sociopolitical problems, since different societies see their scripts as indicative of their own particular identities. It would be difficult indeed to envision a movement to eliminate all these nationalistic attitudes. The emoji code, on the other hand, poses no such threat. It is an add-on code that is seen across the world as enhancing international communications. In other words, the emoji code seems to be achieving the very goals that Blissymbolics has not yet achieved, getting people across the globe at the very least to communicate with each other in a positive way through the pictorial semantics of the code.

The emoji code

The emoji code is an artificial one. But unlike the proposals by Leibniz or Bliss, it is not intended to replace traditional writing scripts; rather, it aims, by and large, to enhance comprehension among speakers of different languages and to add positivity to messages.

It is useful here to list all the characteristics of the emoji code in point form, synthesized from previous chapters:

1 Emoji are standardized picture-words that are used commonly in informal messages of all kinds to add semantic nuances, to emphasize tone, to avoid potential misunderstandings, and to fulfill various phatic and emotive functions; they are not meant to replace existing scripts.

2 They are provided by Unicode and other systems on keyboards, or else they come with different forms via apps and websites. They are thus similar to letters on a keyboard in that they can be selected with a stroke; but they are not phonemic, but rather conceptual, like pictographs. In other words, they are selected for semantic-conceptual reasons, not character-based ones.

3 They are rarely used (if at all) in messages where the tone is serious or reflective; however, as we have seen, they are being used more and more in different kinds of messages, including those intended to threaten someone.

4 Emoji that are put at the end of sentences or even interspersed in sentences may have punctuation functions, replacing periods, commas, and the like, although they add considerably in meaning to the sentence, transcending the perfunctory prosody that punctuation marks often entail.

5   The most common use of emoji is in hybrid writing (text and pictures), although emoji-only writing is gaining some popularity. Emoji translations, however, are so difficult to decipher that they contravene a basic principle of least effort in communication theory and are thus unlikely to spread broadly.

6   Emoji add a kind of "comedic tenor" to messages that assuages message impact by imparting a touch of humor through a cartoon style that also enhances the friendliness of the tone.

7   They possess conceptual structure, being located at specific points in a message, for semantic reinforcement. They also are combined into syntagms to relay larger meanings, and with some words they are used in tandem to form adjacency pairs.

8   They produce what has been called here the thesaurus effect, enfolding all kinds of connotations that reach into both universal or core meaning patterns and culture-sensitive ones.

9   They are examples of metaphorical blends at various levels, from the constitutive micro-level one in their configuration or composition, to their distribution and meaning structure at the macro level.

10 Even though they were meant to provide a universal core lexicon by standardizing organizations, they still generate ambiguities and encase various dilemmas of usage and interpretation, which will probably never be resolved, given the variability and indeterminacy of human expressive, interpretive, and communicative processes.

Many of these aspects can certainly be seen to qualify the emoji code as a quasi-universal one, since it also includes a peripheral component to handle cultural coding and other forms of variation. So, it can be said that its characters fall on a universality scale, from low to high, with the basic facial emoji located at the high end and others, such as those for objects such as golf clubs, at the lower end. As discussed in this book, there are around 1,000 emoji symbols that fall beyond the mid-point of the scale toward the high end; but there are many more that fall on the other half of the scale toward the low end. The latter, as discussed, have been added to the emoji code as a result of pressures from different cultures to meet their specific demands.

The emoji phenomenon has, indirectly, shown that ambiguity may be unavoidable in language or any other representational or communicative code. Unicode refers to the meanings that result from ambiguity as "auxiliary" meanings; but this is not accurate, since they really are connotations that accrue via usage of the emoji signs. The instant signs are used pragmatically, they acquire connotative structure and this leads to ambiguity. If the emoji code is indeed to be construed as a universal script that transcends variability of representation, then ambiguity should not exist within it. As we have seen, even in the core lexicon, ambiguity cannot be tamed, let alone eliminated. In a way, the emoji phenomenon is strong evidence that diversity is a principle of life and that schemes for universal languages are really pipe dreams of highly idealistic individuals, since the operation of the diversity principle cannot be eradicated from human systems such as languages.

Perhaps it is more accurate to say that emoji are products of an increasingly expanding global culture, where a common ground of symbolism is developing and spreading throughout the culture. Emoji usage fits in particularly well with the many popular trends that characterize the global village. Indeed, one of the more popular and "fun" uses of emoji is in the emoji versions of popular songs, as discussed in the previous chapter. Below are two recent examples:

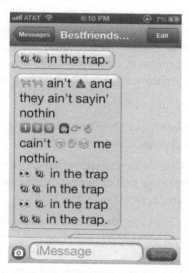

Emoji version of "Bees in the Trap," by Nikki Minaj

Emoji version of "Get Low," by Lil Jon

These uses of emoji suggest that it is a perfect language for a society used to reading cartoons and other hybrid texts. But, more generally, the use of emoji might imply that people in the global village are seeking the expressive means to live in tranquility and happiness. They could thus well be perceived as an antidote to the terror and fear that is spreading throughout the world through conflicts and wars.

Indeed, there are as many conflicts in the world today, if not more so, than in any other previous age. Emoji cannot replace words in the expression of philosophical or scientific ideas. But they can certainly allow common everyday discourse to assume an amicable tinge. Perhaps the emoji movement is, after all, just a momentary trend, as will be discussed in the next chapter, a means to escape from the horrors of the world. The statements of three informants certainly seem to give substance to this assessment:

1   "I love emojis; they put happiness into my life. What a dreary world it would be for me without them."

2   "I would never use emoji in essays that require sophisticated thinking; they're just fine elements that give me a chance to survive in a world of too much hate."

3   "The world is in a mess. Wars everywhere, climate change, depletion of resources. Heck, I need to think positively, at least when I write to my friends. Thank heavens for emoji; they're like comic-book characters. I can laugh and sometimes cry, but never despair when I use them."

10 A COMMUNICATION REVOLUTION?

The digital revolution is far more significant than the invention of writing or even of printing.

DOUGLAS ENGELBART (1925–2013)

Are emoji part of a real revolution in how we communicate or are they just a passing fad? Are they nothing more than "cute" characters that enliven written communication, but have little other value, even when they are used in various domains such as advertising? These are the questions that will be examined in this final chapter—a point of arrival seeking some tangible answer to the meaning of emoji use. Actually, the answer is already in the substance of the interviews with the research informants and in the information gathered for this book. Here it will be extracted from these sources and articulated explicitly.

But before attempting an answer, it is important to take a step back and take a more wide-ranging look at the context and environment in which emoji emerged—the digital universe. As an aside it is relevant to note that ongoing research is starting to suggest that emoji use might have significant effects on neural processes, reshaping the brain. If so, then the answer to the question with which this chapter started is even more critical. Some of the research belabors the obvious, such as the obvious fact that when we see certain emoji, our mood changes. Concomitantly, we alter our facial expressions to match the emotivity of the emoji. Without knowing, we end up mimicking the emoji expression (O'Neill 2013). However, a group of researchers at Tokyo Denki University found that the more graphic the emoji, the more the brain responds to it (Yuasa, Saito, and Mukawa 2011). And this suggests rather concretely that emoji might indeed play a role in shaping cognition and possibly consciousness.

The global village

The emergence of the emoji code as an epigenetic global code is a product of technologies that have facilitated intercultural interactions and which, as some suggest, may have engendered a common or collective consciousness, known vicariously as "connected intelligence," the "global village," or the "global brain," in contrast to the type of consciousness engendered by the Print Age, which can be called the "individualist brain"—a brain that valued privacy, independence of thought from the masses, personal intelligence, difference of opinion from those in authority, and so on. The IQ test is an artifact that perfectly symbolizes the mind-set of the individualist brain—it juxtaposes individual achievement against a standard measure of achievement. The individualist brain is a product of what some have called the "alphabet effect" (Ong 1982; Logan 1986), which claims that the greater economy of alphabet writing and reading requires greater levels of abstraction which, in turn, affect the consciousness of literate users, who, as a consequence, see themselves as distinct from others. I would add that the same effect is evident in pictographic cultures as well. In fact, many of the same cognitive traits found in alphabet users are also evident in pictograph users. It may well be that writing itself (alphabetic, pictographic, and so on) encourages separation from the tribe and cognizance of oneself as autonomous from it.

Whatever the truth, it is obvious that writing does indeed seem to encourage literate people to see themselves as separate individuals and develop a unique sense of Self. Prior to the spread of writing, knowledge was the privilege of the few and literacy was left in the hands of those in power. The growth of literacy substantially reduced the power of those in authority as written texts could be read "individually" and interpretations of their content reached subjectively.

The global village is leading to a continual weakening of the features and values that were characteristic of the individualist brain, replacing them more and more by what can be called the "communal brain." The Print Age encouraged individual readings (literally) of content, not shared meanings. In that Age, literacy became a right and a necessity, not a privilege, as it was in the ancient and medieval worlds. Literacy requires rules of language. Any infringement of these rules is seen as socially inappropriate. But in the Internet Age this situation has changed. The type of language used on social media makes it obvious that the previous rules of literacy have less and less value, evidenced, as we saw, by the fact that orthographic and grammatical perfection are no longer strict requirements for "proper communication."

This does not mean that literacy has disappeared or is drastically undervalued, but rather that its functions in the post-print era have changed. It does not have the premium that it once had. That lasted from the mid-1400s to the late twentieth century. Before the fifteenth century, literacy was not seen as having value nor as a right. Most people in Europe were illiterate, never having had the opportunity, nor seemingly the will, to learn to read and write. There were fewer schools, and books (manuscripts copied by scribes) were scarce and expensive. Literacy was not required to carry out work in farming villages and in the trades of the medieval towns. Most literate people belonged to the nobility, the upper classes, or the clergy. But the printing press changed all this. Through cheap books and other print materials, the written word became the chief means for the propagation and recording of knowledge and ideas. Schooling became increasingly a right, rather than a privilege, since literacy was required by the new workplaces and the new social systems that developed from the Gutenberg revolution.

The printing press set in motion the globalization of knowledge, thus encouraging literacy across the globe. With industry becoming a dominant part of economic life during the eighteenth and nineteenth centuries, great numbers of people started migrating to cities. In order to find employment they had to learn how to read instructions and perform other tasks that required literacy. Governments began to value education more, and systems of public schooling cropped up everywhere. By the late 1800s, formal elementary education had become a virtual necessity.

From this social environment, the individualist brain emerged, which perceives every individual as an independent person who possesses an inalienable right to his or her own opinions, independently of what others think, and independently of authority structures (including laws and established wisdom). Individualism holds that a civilized society can be achieved only on the basis of the recognition of individual rights—and that a collectivity, as such, has no rights other than the set of rights of its individual members. In such societies, the communal (or collective) brain is seen as belonging to a previous stage of human evolution typical of pre-literate societies. If there are "collective thoughts," these are seen as deriving from a consensus of individual thoughts pooled for the common good. All the functions of body and mind are perceived as private. They cannot be shared or transported. In this paradigm, we inherit the ideas of other individuals, but we make of them what we ourselves want or need. We learn from each other, not from specified authority figures or leaders. Individual creativity assumes great importance in such a system, and tribal or communal forms of knowledge are seen as primitive or superstitious.

But in the end, individualism is an ideal, shaped by socio-technological forces. It is a worthy one; but it also has a serious downside. Mental diseases are part of this downside. For this reason, clinical psychology, not religion, has emerged to harmonize the mind with its surroundings. Movements such as psychoanalysis, existentialism, absurdism, surrealism, and postmodernism could never have emerged in a tribal society where the harmony of the group is emphasized; they are products of the individualist brain which is subject to alienation from the group (Marx 1844; Durkheim 1912). It is little wonder that in the Internet Age, where a virtual communal brain is crystallizing, such previous movements and psychological practices hold less sway. In academia, individualism brought about debates and studies on identity, alterity, and other constructs of the individualist brain. Today, these are receding somewhat as the new generation of students is more interested in contact with others through digital media, not separation from them.

When the internet came into wide use, it was heralded as bringing about a liberation from conformity and a channel for expressing one's opinions freely. But this view has proven to be specious. In contrast to the pre-internet print world (Jay 1996), it can be said that internet culture is built on the attainment of a communal consciousness through artificial means. Living in a social media universe, we may indeed feel that it is the only option available to us. The triumph of social media lies in their promise to allow human needs to be expressed individualistically, yet connect them to a common ground—hence the paradox. Moreover, as the communal brain takes shape in the global village, a form of global connected intelligence is emerging, called by some a "global brain."

This term was actually coined before the Internet Age by Peter Russell in his 1983 book, *The Global Brain*, anticipating the effects of new technologies on human consciousness. The concept has, since then, produced a whole series of new theories about humanity that could only crystallize in the electronic universe. One of these is *post-humanism*, used broadly to refer to an era in which humans no longer dominate the world but instead have merged with their machines and with animals to create a new world order that pits humans not at the center of the universe but as equal partners with other intelligences (artificial and animal). A leader of this movement is Donna Haraway (1989, 1991), whose ideas about the impact of technology on our perception of the body have become widely quoted in media, culture, and communication studies. She is also well known for her work on "cyborg theory," or the view that machines are merging more and more with humans, replacing many functions of the human body and mind. But scholars like Haraway are ignoring the paradox of technology. We always tend to retrieve the past in the present, and thus human progress is not linear, but cyclical.

The main claim of global brain theorists is that a single information-learning-communication system is emerging via the internet which functions as if it were a nervous system connecting the entire planet. Intelligence is collective or distributed, not centralized in any particular person, institution, or system. This means that no one individual can control it; the system organizes itself—called *emergence*—from the networks and processes of interaction between the components. The rise and spread of the emoji code can only be understood as a product of emergence; it could only have been devised in a global brain universe, where commonalities are more important than individualities.

This in no way diminishes the creative abilities of individuals; it actually seems to encourage them more as the informants made clear to us. "It all depends on what you mean by creativity," as one informant put it. And this is the paradox of the Internet Age. The internet is one huge network for people to both connect with each other and for individuals to put themselves on display. It was philosopher Pierre Teilhard de Chardin who saw all this coming already in 1945. His term for what is now the internet was the *noosphere*, a cognitive environment which would show the "planetization" of humanity, implying an irreversible and irresistible form of evolution that he called "macrobiological." From this, a "global mind," as he called it, would emerge that no longer is capable of individuating ideas or assigning importance to authorship. De Chardin's theory is often called *cosmogenesis* or *organicism*. It became an obvious source of inspiration for global brain theory, which envisions both individuals and societies as critical subsystems that are interconnected for reasons of species survival. The cliché "two heads are better than one" translates in this framework to "all heads are better than one."

An example of how the communal brain interacts with previous individualism is Wikipedia, which interconnects the resources of the Web with the collective intelligence of its countless contributors. The key here is that authorship is not crucial, and that individuals can glean a sense of importance by the very fact that their ideas are amalgamated into the encyclopedia with those of others. In the end, the concept of global brain is really just an idea; it does not describe an evolutionary paradigm shift in itself; it describes how we now perceive ourselves in the global village. It does not eliminate the individualist brain; it assigns new status to it.

It is important to note, on this point, that both de Chardin and McLuhan saw the possibility of the human spirit being made obsolete because of the enthusiasm over notions such as theirs, and thus both issued a warning that technology and communal brain theories are human creations, not inevitable processes whereby human will is obliterated and human destiny will ineluctably follow a predetermined path. They warned against accepting this kind of determinism. They both maintained that personal choice and free will still allow people to make a difference to the universe. The creation of collective intelligence is exactly that—a creation. It describes how we now communicate, interact, learn, and perceive ourselves; but it does not eliminate choice or the ability of the imagination to change things.

Emoji as trend

As mentioned above, the emoji phenomenon emerges in a global brain universe, constituting a perfect new language for it. But it is not a complete language; it is, as we have seen in this book, an ephemeral one surfacing internationally because of its ease of usage and its many universal semantic properties. But it is also literally a "popular language": that is, it is a language that has many of its symbolic tentacles in pop culture, including areas such as cartoons and comic books, as discussed. Popular forms of language have crystallized constantly throughout modern history, as have certain phrases and discourse styles that became popular through hit songs, movies, jingles, and the like. Pop language allows people to "talk the talk." It is a form of discourse that manifests itself across the modern social landscape, from advertising, sportscasting, and movie trailers to news headlines. Most people would call pop language slang. But this is incorrect. It is an informal code that comes from trends in popular culture, not from in-group linguistic conventions.

The term pop language was introduced by journalist Leslie Savan in her book, *Slam Dunks and No-Brainers: Language in Your Life, the Media, Business, Politics, and, Like, Whatever* (2005), to describe the kind of language that is used in popular spectacles and texts, spreading throughout society through the media and reinforced by marketplace forces. Throughout society, Savan notes, people are using a style of speech, which carries with it a built-in "applause sign" or "laugh track." Phrases such as "That is so last year"; "Don't go there"; "Get a life"; "I hate it when that happens"; "It doesn't get any better than this"; and the sneering "I don't think so" come from television sitcoms and popular movies and have spread broadly to other media, migrating to everyday speech habits. Pop language is unconsciously attractive, claims Savan, because it emanates from popular media and is thus felt to be "hip" and in sync with the times. Like sitcom dialogue, it is light, self-conscious, ironic, and replete with put-downs, catchy phrases, and exaggerated inflections. Does the emoji code fit in with this characterization? At one level, it certainly would seem to—it expresses the new global voice of pop culture in an effective way. It is also anti-hegemonic, as argued previously, satirizing the boredom of serious talk. It allows for the comedic side of the human mind to express itself without reprobation. In this sense, it is actually a kind of therapeutic language, rather than senseless verbiage. We asked our informants the following question: "Does emoji writing make you feel more comfortable when communicating, reducing the stress of face-to-face interactions?" Everyone interviewed answered this in the affirmative. One informant actually used the word "therapeutic" to describe the feeling she experienced when choosing and inserting emoji in her texts. It is an emotional facilitator language, so to speak, since it allows amusing images to color the interaction as well as bolster its semantic structure. It is both a form of communication and of entertainment. For this reason, it has social and emotive resonance. In so doing it provides insights into modern society and its values, fears, and trends.

Perhaps, the emoji code is part of an evolutionary thrust to make languages much more comprehensible to the global brain. The history of English shows a constant flow toward simplification and comprehensibility. As discussed previously, all one has to do is look at the writings of Chaucer or Shakespeare to realize the extent to which English has changed over the years. Many of the actual features of pop-language spelling today are the same ones proposed by many in the past. In 1828, Noah Webster proposed the elimination of *u* in words such as *colour, harbour, favour,* and *odour*. His proposal was accepted, and the resulting spelling difference is a feature that distinguishes American from British English—and that, by extension, divides America from its British past. Changes of this kind have always come about to symbolize a break with tradition. American English itself was once considered to be subversive by the British (since it was not the King's English). In some ways, therefore, new writing styles such as emoji style are popular in America because they are part of a larger tendency in that country to constantly break from the past. As Vivian Cook (2004: viii) has perceptively remarked:

> Our discussions of spelling often suggest that there is an ideal of perfect spelling that people should strive for. Correct spelling and punctuation are seen as injunctions carved on tablets of stone; to break them is to transgress the tacit commandments for civilized behavior. Spelling and punctuation can become an emotional rather than rational area of dispute.

In her 2011 master's thesis at the University of Calgary, *What Does Txting do 2 Language*, Joan H. Lee argues that exposure to and use of pop language leads to a diminution in people's acceptance of vocabulary, thus reducing it considerably. Lee discovered that students with more exposure to traditional print media (books and articles) were more open to expanding their vocabulary. "Our assumption about texting is that it encourages unconstrained language," Lee argues, "but the study found this to be a myth." Lee suggests that reading traditional print materials exposes people to linguistic variety and creativity that is not found in pop language and thus, by deduction, in the emoji code.

Of course, Lee is referring to different forms of creativity—the creativity of a Dostoyevsky cannot be compared to the creativity of a Twitter user. What needs to be seen is what literary genres will emerge, if any, from hybrid writing, and if they will stand up to traditional literary texts. As we saw in previous chapters, entire texts are now being written in emoji. But so far they have not become popular or relevant as traditional novels have. The informants in our research group shed very significant light on the uses and importance of literacy practices today. Overall, one can glean from their responses that there is an awareness of the need for two literacies—one for informal digital communications and one for the traditional Print Age goals of education and science. Some of their responses are reproduced below:

1. "I would never use emoji in serious writing; it's really just a way of bonding with others."
2. "I know when to use them and when not."
3. "I prefer them to the abbreviations; they have more meaning. I have difficulty writing essays without them, but I know that I have to try."
4. "It's just a fun language; there's no fun in essays and science, right?"
5. "I never use emoji outside of my family and friends."

Emoji is a playful and entertaining language. It is evolving epigenetically, unlike other artificial languages, thus bringing it closer and closer to natural languages in its evolutionary propensities. It is a fluid, organic form of language, and the meanings of emoji symbols are now interpreted differently and applied differently within certain cultures. People have adopted entirely new uses and meanings for them. Essentially, emoji enhance or clarify the meaning and context of a written message in the absence of such cues as vocal intonation and register, hand gestures, and facial expressions. Overall, as we have seen, emoji express "tone of voice" in a medium that has no tone of voice. It serves as emotional punctuation, amplification, adding context, wordplay, nuance, and thus allowing interlocutors to speak their minds while taking the edge off their messages.

One informant made the following truly significant statement: "I can sum up emoji in one word: fun." He exemplified his assessment by illustrating to the interviewers the emoji he would use when he wanted to convey that he was drunk to a friend:

"Drunk" emoji

If the message was a warning, he would use the following emoji to accompany a phrase such as "Oops, you're gonna be sorry":

"You're gonna be sorry" emoji

Another informant actually gave us a very interesting insight, pointing out that the most commonly used emoji are really basic speech protocols or visual annotations on what is occurring semantically and discursively during a text conversation. She gave the following list as the most common ones, in her opinion, at least. Incidentally, we found that these were consistent with online assessments and with new keyboard configurations:

Be quiet! This corresponds to the metaphor "Zip your mouth."	
Bombshell This is a blend of bomb + shell, producing the emoji word.	
Call me! This emoji is designed to imitate the common gesture indicating the use of a phone.	
Drama queen As we have seen, this is also used as a "princess" signature.	

Good luck! As already discussed, this blend of the "thumbs-up" and "four-leaf clover" emoji is self-explanatory.	👍 🍀
Rock star/Rock on! This emoji stands for the "rock on" gesture.	🤘
Screw you! This is the emoji version of the "middle finger" gesture.	🖕
See you soon! As discussed previously, this is the waving-hand emoji, constituting a salutation protocol.	👋
Smoking hot Clearly, this blend of the cigarette emoji (for *smoking*) and the fire emoji (for *hot*) produces the appropriate meaning.	🚬 🔥

Common emoji

As discussed, a specific kind of pragmatic competence is involved here which is a very pliable one, clearly, and it does not interfere with other competencies which are more akin to the traditional literacy ones of the past. In a phrase, emoji writing is in no way interfering with other more formal registers of writing, at least as far as can be told. It is a "lingo," as another informant described it, "that is fun and easy to use."

The future of emoji

Every book needs a conclusion. But in this case, it is difficult to find one. The present study of emoji has entailed a collage of ideas and research findings, mirroring the collage that characterizes the emoji code itself.

If there is a conclusion to this descriptive foray into this new form of writing, it is an elusive one that can best be articulated as a rhetorical question: Is emoji writing a passing trend or is it truly a new form of global writing?

For one thing, it arises in the context of a growing use of visuality in representational and communicative practices in a global brain environment. But unlike, say, Blissymbolics, it does not have a closed system of rules for usage and construction; it is a substitutive form of script that adds nuance and tone to textual writing, providing emotive, phatic, and rhetorical force to it. It thus adds utterance meaning to textual writing. Several of the themes that have emerged during the course of the analysis are worth reiterating here in summary form:

1   The main use of emoji is in informal messages typically shared among acquaintances, friends, and others with whom the informal register applies. Their use extends to various online venues, such as Twitter, Instagram, dating websites, as well as domains such as advertising and politics.

2   Because the emoji are provided by standardized systems such as Unicode, they essentially constitute a visual alphabet, allowing users to insert the images in texts structurally, conceptually, and pragmatically: they have virtually replaced previous salutation and punctuation forms of informal written texts.

3   The most common, and communicatively effective, use of emoji is in hybrid writing. This allows for the distribution of the images to be guided by the conceptual flow of a message, whereby emoji are inserted in locations to emphasize the meaning of some word or phrase, or else, as markers of emotional pauses.

4   Attempts at emoji-only writing (as in the translation of entire books or in advertising messages) have not become widespread, since they arguably require too much effort to decode.

5   The emoji code is thus used primarily in an adjunctive way, much like the rebus and illuminated writing practices of the past, wherein images were used to allow for both a better understanding of the content or to make annotations and enhancements to the tone of the written text. They also are used for satirical or ironic purposes.

6   As the research team found, emoji are mood enhancers, allowing for a friendly tone to be established or maintained, thus reducing the risk of conflict that can otherwise arise, as in F2F conversations.

7   The emoji code amplifies writing practices considerably, retrieving pictographic and illuminative practices of the past in new ways. But this does not render phonetic alphabets obsolescent; rather it allows users to reflect upon hybrid writing as related to other modes of writing, such as the more serious and philosophical ones.

8   Emoji fit in with the concept of the "save-a-keystroke principle," perhaps reflecting the fact that we have reached the limit of abbreviating written words and expressions.

9   The emoji code can be divided into two sections—a core lexicon and a peripheral lexicon. The former is the one that is higher up on the universality scale; the latter reflects the variation introduced into the emoji code from cross-cultural usage.

10 Critiques against emoji writing stem from the perception of writing characteristic of the Print Age literacies and the implicit perspective that complexity of thought is connected to complexity of writing. This may well be for specific uses of language such as in philosophy, but it is not a law of cognition. In mathematics, for example, it is compression (into formulas and equations) that characterizes complexity, not elaborate explanations.

11 Overall, the emoji code has resurrected visuality in phonetic writing, albeit in a new way, allowing our eyes to recapture the visual modality that was there in early writing systems.

12 Overall, though, the emoji code constitutes a form of pop language that conveys humor, friendliness, laughter, and fun in a systematic way. It is not a coincidence that the emoji code was originally inspired by Manga comics.

Emoji writing was prefigured in movements such as Dada, futurism, and perhaps even writers such as e. e. cummings who wrote in lower case, and used distortions of syntax, unusual punctuation, new words, elements of slang, eliminating spaces, and using visual forms throughout (such as slanting his poem to represent the form of the animal or idea he was describing). Emoji is arguably the latest manifestation of a modern-day tendency to reform writing to be more reflective of other modalities than the strictly phonetic one. It is a cartoon form of writing that keeps us entertained and away from the real problems of the world. This is, actually, how cummings himself characterized the tabloid newspaper (cited by *Vanity Fair*, December 1926): "The tabloid newspaper actually means to the typical American what the Bible is popularly supposed to have meant to the typical Pilgrim Father: a very present help in times of trouble, plus a means of keeping out of trouble via harmless, since vicarious, indulgence in the pomps and vanities of this wicked world."

So, is the rise and spread of emoji a passing trend or the arrival of a veritable new universal language? This is the question presented in the preface of this book and at the start of this chapter. But there really is no clear answer. In the global village trends come and go quickly and this could easily be one of them. As one informant told us, with the growth of voice-activated technologies which might eventually replace keyboard communication, the era of emoji may come to pass as new forms of orality interface with visuality. So, to conclude—there is no conclusion. In my own estimation, it is highly probable that the emoji phenomenon is an ephemeral one that will recede as new technologies come forward and as new needs arise in the global village, just as our informant stated. Human communicative systems are highly adaptable and adaptive, capable of responding to changes in the world and in human consciousness, indeed often becoming dynamically intertwined with them. It is thus fitting to end with a quotation from the contemporary writer Douglas Adams, who expresses the relation between technologies and forms of representation cleverly as follows:

"First we thought the PC was a calculator. Then we found out how to turn numbers into letters with ASCII—and we thought it was a typewriter. Then we discovered graphics, and we thought it was a television. With the World Wide Web, we've realized it's a brochure."

REFERENCES

Alexander, James (2012). "On the Cognitive and Semiotic Structure of Mathematics." In M. Bockarova, M. Danesi, and R. Núñez (eds.), *Semiotic and Cognitive Science Essays on the Nature of Mathematics*, 1–34. Munich: Lincom Europa.

Arnheim, Rudolph (1969). *Visual Thinking*. Berkeley: University of California Press.

Auletta, Ken (2008). *Googled: The End of the World as We Know It*. New York: Penguin.

Austin, John L. (1961). *How to Do Things with Words*. Cambridge, MA: Harvard University Press.

Azuma, Junichi and Ebner, Martin (2008). "Stylistic Analysis of Graphic Emoticons: Can They be Candidates for a Universal Visual Language of the Future?" In J. Luca and E. R. Weippl (eds.), *World Conference on Educational Media and Technology*. Vienna, Austria: Association for the Advancement of Computing in Education (AACE). http://editlib.org/p/28510.

Bar–Hillel, Yehoshua. 1960. "The Present Status of Automatic Translation of Languages." *Advances in Computers* 1: 91–163.

Baron, Naomi (2008). *Always On*. Oxford: Oxford University Press.

Barthes, Roland (1964). "Rhetoric of the Image." In Carolyn Handa (ed.), *Visual Rhetoric in a Visual World: A Critical Sourcebook*. 152–63. New York: Bedford/St. Martin's.

Barthes, Roland (1977). *Image-Music-Text*. London: Fontana.

Barthes, Roland (1981). *Camera Lucida*. New York: Hill and Wang.

Barthes, Roland and Lavers, Annette (1968). *Elements of Semiology*. New York: Hill and Wang.

Baudrillard, Jean (983). *Simulations*. New York: Semiotexte.

Bergen, Benjamin (2001). "Nativization Processes in L1 Esperanto." *Journal of Child Language* 28: 575–95.

Birdwhistell, Ray L. (1952). *Introduction to Kinesics*. Ann Arbor, MI: University of Ann Arbor.

Bliss, Charles K. (1949). *International Semantography: A Non-Alphabetical Symbol Writing Readable in All Languages. A Practical Tool for General International Communication, Especially in Science, Industry, Commerce, Traffic, etc. and for Semantical Education, Based on the Principles of Ideographic Writing and Chemical Symbolism*. Sydney: Institute of Semantography.

Bliss, Charles K. (1955). *Semantography and the Ultimate Meanings of Mankind: Report and Reflections on a Meeting of the Author with Julian Huxley. A selection of the Semantography Series; with "What scientists think of C.K. Bliss' semantography."* Sydney: Institute of Semantography.

Bliss, Charles K. (1978). *Semantography-Blissymbolics: A Simple System of 100 Logical Pictorial Symbols, Which can be Operated and Read Like 1+2=3 in All Languages.* Sydney: Semantography-Blissymbolics Pubs.

Bliss, Charles K. (1985). *The Blissymbols Picture Book (Three Volumes), Development and Advisory Publications of N.S.W. for Semantography-Blissymbols.* Coogee: Institute of Semantography.

Bloomfield, Leonard (1933). *Language.* New York: Holt.

Blot, Richard K. (ed.) (2003). *Language and Social Identity.* Westport: Praeger.

Bogdan, Catalina (2002). *The Semiotics of Visual Languages.* New York: Columbia University Press.

Bouissac, Paul (1993). "Beyond Style: Steps towards a Semiotic Hypothesis." In M. Lorblanchet and P. G. Bahn (eds.), *Rock Art Studies: The Post-Stylistic Era,* 203–06. Oxford: Oxbow Monograph 35.

Bouissac, Paul (1994). "Art or Script? A Falsifiable Semiotic Hypothesis." *Semiotica* 100 (2–4): 349–67; "Introduction: A Challenge for Semiotics." *Semiotica* 100 (2–4): 99–107.

Bouissac, Paul (1997). "New Epistemological Perspectives for the Archaeology of Writing." In I. R. Blench and N. Spriggs (eds.), *Archaeology and Language,* 53–62. London: Routledge.

Bouissac, Paul (1999). "The Semiotics of Facial Transformations and the Construction of Performing Identities." *Journal of Comparative Cultures* 3: 1–17.

Bouissac, Paul (2010). *Saussure: A Guide for the Perplexed.* London: Bloomsbury.

Bower, Gordon H. (1980). *Theories of Learning,* 5th ed. Boston: Pearson.Brown, Penelope and Levinson, Stephen (1987).

Carlyle, Thomas (1841). *On Heroes.* London: James Fraser.

Carr, Caleb, Schrock, David, and Dauterman, Patricia (2012). "Speech Acts within Facebook Status Messages." *Journal of Language and Social Psychology* 31: 176–96.

Carr, Nicholas (2008). *The Shallows: What the Internet is Doing to our Brains.* New York: Norton.

Cattuto, Ciro, Loreto, Vittorio, and Pietronero, Luciano (2007). "Semiotic Dynamics and Collaborative Tagging." *Proceedings of the national Academy of Sciences of America* 104: 1461–64.

Céard, Jean (1986). *Rébus de la Renaissance: des images qui parlent.* Paris: Maisonneuve et Larose.

Chardin, Pierre Teilhard de (1945) [2008]. *The Phenomenon of Man.* New York: Harper.

Cherry, Colin (1957). *On Human Communication.* Cambridge, MA: MIT Press.

Cohen, C. Jonathan. (1954). "On the Project of a Universal Character." *Mind (New Series)* 63: 249.

Cohn, Neil (2013). *The Visual Language of Comics: Introduction to the Structure and Cognition of Sequential Images*. London: Bloomsbury.

Collister, Lauren (2015). "Textspeak is Modernizing the English Language." *New Republic*. https://newrepublic.com/article/121463/textspeak-streamlining-language-not-ruining-it.

Cook, Vivian (2004). *Why Can't Anybody Spell?* New York: Touchstone.

Coulmas, Florian (1989). *The Writing Systems of the World*. Oxford: Blackwell.

Crystal, David (2006). *Language and the Internet*, 2nd ed. Cambridge: Cambridge University Press.

Crystal, David (2008). *txtng: the gr8 db8*. Oxford: Oxford University Press.

Crystal, David (2011). *Internet Linguistics*. New York: Routledge.

Cunliffe, Daniel, Morris, Delyth, and Prys, Cynog (2013). "Young Bilinguals' Language Behaviour in Social Networking Sites: The Use of Welsh on Facebook." *Journal of Computer-Mediated Communication* 18 (3): 339–61.

Danescu-Niculescu-Mizil, Cristian, Gamon, Michael, and Dumais, Susan (2011). Mark My Words! Linguistic Style Accommodation in Social Media. *International World Wide Web Conference Committee*, ACM 978-1-4503-0632-4/11/03.

Danesi, Marcel (1994). *Cool: The Signs and Meanings of Adolescence*. Toronto: University of Toronto Press.

Danesi, Marcel (2011). "George Lakoff on the Cognitive and Neural Foundation of Mathematics." *Fields Notes* 11 (3): 14–20.

Danesi, Marcel (2013). "On the Metaphorical Connectivity of Cultural Sign Systems." *Signs and Society* 1: 33–50.

Danesi, Marcel (2016). *Language and Mathematics: An Interdisciplinary Perspective*. Berlin: Mouton de Gruyter.

Danesi, Marcel and Perron, Paul (1999). *Analyzing Cultures*. Bloomington: Indiana University Press.

Danesi, Marcel and Rocci, Andrea (2009). *Global Linguistics*. Berlin: Mouton de Gruyter.

Danet, Brenda and Herring, Susan C. (eds.) (2007). *The Multilingual Internet: Language, Culture, and Communication Online*. Oxford: Oxford University Press.

Darley, Andrew (2000). *Visual Digital Culture: Surface Play and Spectacle in Media Genres*. London: Routledge.

Darwin, Charles (1872). *The Expression of the Emotions in Man and Animals*. Chicago: University of Chicago Press.

Deregowski, Jan B. (1982). "Pictorial Perception and Culture." *Scientific American* 227: 82–88.

Derrida, Jacques (1976). *Of Grammatology*. Translated by G. C. Spivak. Baltimore: Johns Hopkins Press.

Dillon, George L. (1999). *Art and the Semiotics of Images: Three Questions About Visual Meaning*. University of Birmingham, July 1999.

Diringer, David (1962). *The Alphabet, A Key to the History of Mankind*, 2nd ed. New York: Philosophical Library.

Dondis, Donis A. (1986). *A Primer of Visual Literacy*. Cambridge, MA: MIT Press.

Drucker, Johanna (2014). *Graphesis: Visual Forms of Knowledge Production*. Cambridge, MA: Harvard University Press.

Dunning, William V. (1991). *Changing Images of Pictorial Space: A History of Visual Illusion in Painting*. Syracuse: Syracuse University Press.

Dutton, Dennis (2010). *The Art Instinct: Beauty, Pleasure, and Human Evolution*. London: Bloomsbury.

Eco, Umberto (1976). *A Theory of Semiotics*. Bloomington: Indiana University Press.

Eco, Umberto (1992). *Interpretation and Overinterpretation*. Cambridge: Cambridge University Press.

Ekman, Paul (1973). *Darwin and Facial Expression: A Century of Research in Review*. New York: Academic.

Ekman, Paul (1976). "Movements with Precise Meanings." *Journal of Communication* 26: 14–26.

Ekman, Paul (1980). "The Classes of Nonverbal Behavior." In W. Raffler-Engel (ed.), *Aspects of Nonverbal Communication*, 89–102. Lisse: Swets and Zeitlinger.

Ekman, Paul (1982). "Methods for Measuring Facial Action." In K. R. Scherer and P. Ekman (eds.), *Handbook of Methods in Nonverbal Behavior*, 45–90. Cambridge: Cambridge University Press.

Ekman, Paul (1985). *Telling Lies*. New York: Norton.

Ekman, Paul (2003). *Emotions Revealed*. New York: Holt.

Ekman, Paul and Friesen, Wallace (1975). *Unmasking the Face*. Englewood Cliffs: Prentice-Hall.

Fauconnier, Gilles and Turner, Mark (2002). *The Way We Think: Conceptual Blending and the Mind's Hidden Complexities*. New York: Basic.

Ferrero, Guillaume (1894). "L'inertie mentale et la loi du moindre effort." *Revue Philosophique de la France et de l'Étranger* 37: 169–82.

Foss, Sonja K. (2005). "Theory of Visual Rhetoric." In Ken Smith, Sandra Moriarity, Gretchen Barbatsis, and Keith Kenney (eds.), *Handbook of Visual Communication: Theory, Methods, and Media*, 141–52. London: Routledge.

Foucault, Michel (1972). *The Archeology of Knowledge*. Translated by A. M. Sheridan Smith. New York: Pantheon.

Gilbert, Eric and Karahalios, Karrie (2009). "Predicting Tie Strength with Social Media." In *Proceedings of the SIGCHI Conference on Human Factors in Computing Systems*, 211–20. New York: ACM.

Gitlin, Todd (2001). *Media Unlimited: How the Torrent of Images and Sounds Overwhelms Out Lives*. New York: Picador.

Goffman, Erving (1955). "On Face-Work: An Analysis of Ritual Elements in Social Interaction." *Psychiatry: Journal for the Study of International Processes* 18: 213–31.

Goffman, Erving (1974). *Frame Analysis*. Cambridge, MA: Harvard University Press.

Goldwasser (1995). *From Icon to Metaphor: Studies in the Semiotics of the Hieroglyphs*. Freiburg: Universtätsverlag.

Goodwin, Charles and Goodwin, Marjorie (1992). "Assessments and the Construction of Context." In A. Duranti and C. Goodwin (eds.), *Rethinking Context: Language as an Interactive Phenomenon*. 1–13. Cambridge: Cambridge University Press.

Gramsci, Antonio (1931). *Lettere dal carcere*. Torino: Einaudi.

Grice, H. Paul (1975). "Logic and Conversation." In P. Cole and J. Morgan (eds.), *Syntax and Semantics*, Vol. 3, 41–58. New York: Academic.

Group μ (1970). *A General Rhetoric*. Paris: Larousse.

Group μ (1992). *Traité du signe visuel: Pour une rhétorique de l'image*. Paris: Seuil.

Halliday, M. A. K. (1985). *Introduction to Functional Grammar*. London: Arnold.

Handa, Carolyn (2004). *Visual Rhetoric in a Digital World: A Critical Sourcebook*. New York: Bedford/St. Martin's.Hariman and Lucaitis 2011.

Haraway, Donna (1989). *Primate Visions: Gender, Race and Nature in the World of Modern Science*. London: Routledge.

Haraway, Donna (1991). *Simians, Cyborgs, and Women: The Reinvention of Nature*. London: Free Association Books.

Helprin, Mark (2009). *Digital Barbarism: A Writer's Manifesto*. New York: Harper Collins.

Heussen, Yana, Binkofski, Ferdinand, and Jolij, Jacob (2011). "The Semantics of the Lying Face." *International Journal of Psychophysiology* 77: 206–07.

Hill, Charles A. and Helmers, Marguerite (eds.) (2004). *Defining Visual Rhetorics*. Mahwah: Lawrence Erlbaum.

Hoffman, Barry (2002). *The Fine Art of Advertising*. New York: Stewart, Tabori & Chang.

Huang, Albert H., Yen, David C. and Zhang, Xiaoni (2008). "Exploring Potential Effects of Emoticons." *Information & Management* 45: 466–73.

Hymes, Dell (1971). *On Communicative Competence*. Philadelphia: University of Pennsylvania Press.

Ingram, David. (1978). "Typology and Universals of Personal Pronouns." In J. H. Greenberg (ed.), *Universals of Human Language*, 213–47. Stanford: Stanford University Press.

Jakobson, Roman (1960). "Linguistics and Poetics." In T. A. Sebeok (ed.), *Style and Language*, 34–45. Cambridge, MA: MIT Press.

Jappy, Tony (2013). *Introduction to Peircean Visual Semiotics*. London: Bloomsbury.

Johnson, Mark (1987). *The Body in the Mind: The Bodily Basis of Meaning, Imagination and Reason*. Chicago: University of Chicago Press.

Kosslyn, Stephen M. (1983). *Ghosts in the Mind's Machine: Creating and Using Images in the Brain*. New York: W. W. Norton.

Kosslyn, Stephen M. (1994). *Image and Brain*. Cambridge, MA: MIT Press.

Laitman, J. T. (1983). "The Evolution of the Hominid Upper Respiratory System and Implications for the Origins of Speech." In E. de Grolier (ed.),

Glossogenetics: The Origin and Evolution of Language, 63–90. Utrecht: Harwood.

Laitman, J. T. (1990). "Tracing the Origins of Human Speech." In P. Whitten and D. E. K. Hunter (eds.), *Anthropology: Contemporary Perspectives*, 124–30. Glenview, IL: Scott, Foresman and Company.

Lakoff, George (1987). *Women, Fire and Dangerous Things: What Categories Reveal about the Mind*. Chicago: University of Chicago Press.

Lakoff, George (2012). "The Contemporary Theory of Metaphor." In M. Danesi and S. Maida–Nicol (eds.), *Foundational Texts in Linguistic Anthropology*, 128–71. Toronto: Canadian Scholars' Press.

Lakoff, George and Johnson, Mark (1980). *Metaphors We Live By*. Chicago: University of Chicago Press.

Langacker, Ronald (1987). *Foundations of Cognitive Grammar*. Stanford: Stanford University Press.

Langer, Suzanne K. (1948). *Philosophy in a New Key*. New York: Mentor Books.

Leibniz, Gottried Willhelm (1966). *Zur allgemeinen Charakteristik. Hauptschriften zur Grundlegung der Philosophie. Philosophische Werke Band 1. Übersetzt von Artur Buchenau. Durchgesehen und mit Einleitungen und Erläuterungen herausgegeben von Ernst Cassirer*. Hamburg: Felix Meiner Verlag GmbH.

Lillis, Theresa (2013). *The Sociolinguistics of Writing*. Edinburgh: Edinburgh University Press.

Logan, Robert K. (1986). *The Alphabet Effect*. New York: William Morrow.

Ma, Xiaoyue and Cahier, Jean-Pierre (2014). "Graphically Structured Icons for Knowledge Tagging." *Journal of Information Science* 40: 779–95.

Malinowski, Bronislaw (1923). "The Problem of Meaning in Primitive Languages." In C. K. Ogden and I. A. Richards (eds.), *The Meaning of Meaning*, 296–336. New York: Harcourt, Brace and World.

Mallery, Garrick (1972). *Sign Language among North American Indians Compared with That Among Other Peoples and Deaf-mutes*. The Hague: Mouton.

Mandelbrot, Benoit (1954). "Structure formelle des textes et communication." *Word* 10: 1–27.

Mandelbrot, Benoit (1977). *The Fractal Geometry of Nature*. New York: Freeman and Co.

Martinet, André (1955). *Économie des changements phonétiques*. Paris: Maisonneuve and Larose.

McLuhan, Marshall (1962). *The Gutenberg Galaxy: The Making of Typographic Man*. Toronto: University of Toronto Press.

McLuhan, Marshall (1964). *Understanding Media: The Extensions of Man*. London: Routledge.

Mead, Margaret (1964). *Continuities in Cultural Evolution*. New Haven: Yale University Press.

Meyer, Pamela (2010). *Liespotting: Proven Techniques to Detect Deception*. New York: St. Martin's.

Moriarity, Sandra E. (2005). "Visual Semiotics Theory." In Ken Smith, Sandra Moriarity, Gretchen Barbatsis, and Keith Kenney (eds.), *Handbook of Visual Communication: Theory, Methods, and Media*, 227–41. London: Routledge.

Morris, Charles W. (1938). *Foundations of the Theory of Signs*. Chicago: University of Chicago Press.

Morris, Charles W. (1946). *Writings on the General Theory of Signs*. The Hague: Mouton.

Morris, Desmond, Collett, Peter, Marsh, Peter, and O'Shaughnessy, Mari (1979). *Gestures: Their Origins and Distributions*. London: Cape.

Nazir, Bairrah (2012). "Gender Patterns on Facebook: A Sociolinguistic Perspective." *International Journal of Linguistics* 4: 252–65.

Novak, Petra Kralj, Smailović, Jasmina, Sluban, Borut, and Mozetič, Igor (2015). "Sentiment of Emojis." *PLoS ONE* 10 (12): e0144296. doi:10.1371/journal. pone.0144296.

O'Neill, Brittney (2013). "Mirror, Mirror on the Screen, What Does All this ASCII Mean?: A Pilot Study of Spontaneous Facial Mirroring of Emotions." *The Arbitus Review* 4: http://journals.uvic.ca/index.php/arbutus/article/view/12681.

Olson, David (1977). *Media and Symbols: The Forms of Expression, Communication and Education*. Chicago: University of Chicago Press.

Olson, Lester C. and Finnegan, Cara A. (eds.) (2008). *Visual Rhetoric: A Reader in Communication and American Culture*. London: Sage.

Ong, Walter (1982). *Orality and Literacy*. New York: Methuen.

Paolillo, John C. (2001). "Language Variation on Internet Relay Chat: A Social Network Approach." *Journal of Sociolinguistics* 5: 180–213.

Peck, Stephen R. (1987). *Atlas of Facial Expression*. Oxford: Oxford University Press.

Peirce, Charles S. (1931–58). *Collected Papers of Charles Sanders Peirce*, Vols. 1–8. Edited by C. Hartshorne and P. Weiss. Cambridge, MA: Harvard University Press.

Pérez-Sabater, Carmen (2012). "The Linguistics of Social Networking: A Study of Writing Conventions on Facebook." *Linguistik Online 56*. linguistik-online.de/56.

Petitot, Jean (2010). "Structuralism and Post-structuralism." In T. A. Sebeok and M. Danesi (eds.), *Encyclopedic Dictionary of Semiotics*, 3rd ed., Vol. 3, 1016–53. Berlin: Mouton de Gruyter.

Piaget, Jean (1936). *La naissance de l'intelligence chez l'enfant*. Neuchâtel: Delachaux et Niestlé.

Radcliffe-Brown, Alfred R. (1922). *The Andaman Islanders*. Cambridge: Cambridge University Press.

Ramage, Daniel, Dumais, Susan, and Liebling, Dan (2010). "Characterizing Microblogs with Topic Models." In *International AAAI Conference on Weblogs and Social Media*, 130–37. Association for the Advancement of Artificial Intelligence.

Rampley, Matthew (2005). *Exploring Visual Culture*. Edinburgh: Edinburgh University Press.

Russell, Peter (1983). *The Global Brain*. New York: Tarcher.

Sacks, Harvey, Jefferson, Gail, and Schegloff, Emmanuel A. (1995). *Lectures on Conversation*. Oxford: Blackwell.

Saenger, Paul (1997). *Space Between Words: The Origins of Silent Reading.* Stanford, CA: Stanford University Press.

Saint-Martin, Fernande (1991). *Semiotics of Visual Language.* Bloomington: Indiana University Press.

Santaella-Braga, M. Lucia (1988). "For a Classification of Visual Signs." *Semiotica* 70: 59–78.

Sapir, Edward (1921). *Language.* New York: Harcourt, Brace, and World.

Saussure, Ferdinand de (1916). *Cours de linguistique générale.* Paris: Payot.

Savan, Leslie (2005). *Slam Dunks and No-Brainers: Language in Your Life, the Media, Business, Politics, and, Like, Whatever.* New York: Alfred A. Knopf.

Schmandt-Besserat, Denise (1978). "The Earliest Precursor of Writing." *Scientific American* 238: 50–59. *Pennsylvania Working Papers in Linguistics.*

Schnoebelen, Tyler (2012). Do You Smile with Your Nose? Stylistic Variation in Twitter Emoticons. 18: http://repository.upenn.edu/pwpl/.

Schnoebelen, Tyler (2014). The Grammar of Emoji. idibon.com/the-grammar-of-emoji/.

Schwartz, H. A., et al. (2013). "Personality, Gender, and Age in the Language of Social Media: The Open-Vocabulary Approach." *PLoS ONE* 8: 1–15.

Searle, John R. (1969). *Speech Acts: An Essay in the Philosophy of Language.* Cambridge: Cambridge University Press.

Sebeok, Thomas A. and Danesi, Marcel (2000). *The Forms of Meaning: Modeling Systems Theory and Semiotics.* Berlin: Mouton de Gruyter.

Sebeok, Thomas A. and Umiker-Sebeok, Jean (eds.) (1994). *Advances in Visual Semiotics.* Berlin: Mouton de Gruyter.

Sebeok, Thomas A., Bouissac, Paul, and Herzfeld, Micahel (1986). *Iconicity: Essays on the Nature of Culture.* Amsterdam: John Benjamins.

Selfe, Cynthia (1999). *Technology and Literacy in the Twenty-First Century.* Carbondale: Southern Illinois University Press.

Sonesson, Göran (1989). *Pictorial Concepts: Inquiries into the Semiotic Heritage and its Relevance for the Analysis of the Visual World.* Lund: Lund University Press.

Sonesson, Göran (1994). "Pictorial Semiotics, Gestalt Psychology, and the Ecology of Perception." *Semiotica* 100: 267–331.

Stark, Luke and Crawford, Kate (2015). "The Conservatism of Emoji: Work, Affect, and Communication." *Social Media + Society.* doi: 10.1177/2056305115604853.

Swadesh, Morris (1951). "Diffusional Cumulation and Archaic Residue as Historical Explanations." *Southwestern Journal of Anthropology* 7: 1–21.

Swadesh, Morris (1959). "Linguistics as an Instrument of Prehistory." *Southwestern Journal of Anthropology* 15: 20–35.

Swadesh, Morris (1971). *The Origins and Diversification of Language.* Chicago: Aldine-Atherton.

Tilley, Christopher (1999). *Metaphor and Material Culture.* Oxford: Blackwell.

Titone, Renzo (1977). "A Humanistic Approach to Language Behavior and Language Learning." *Canadian Modern Language Review* 33: 309–17.

Tomaselli, Keyan. (2009). *Appropriating Images: The Semiotics of Visual Representation*. Højbjerg: Intervention Press.

Tomkins, Silvan and Izard, Carroll E. (1965). *Affect, Cognition, and Personality: Empirical Studies*. New York: Springer.

Trager, G. L. (1972). "Writing and Writing Systems." In T. A. Sebeok (ed.), *Current Trends in Linguistics, Vol. 12: Linguistics and Adjacent Arts and Sciences*, 373–96. The Hague: Mouton.

Turner, Mark (2012). "Mental Packing and Unpacking in Mathematics." In Mariana Bockarova, Marcel Danesi, and Rafael Núñez (eds.), *Semiotic and Cognitive Science Essays on the Nature of Mathematics*, 123–34. Munich: Lincom Europa.

Uspenskij, Boris (2001). *La pala d'altare di Jan van Eyck a Gand: La composizione dell'opera (la prospettiva divina e la prospettiva umana)*. Milano: Lupetti.

Vaidhyanathan, Siva (2011). *The Googlization of Everything (and Why We Should Worry)*. Berkeley: University of California Press.

Vygotsky, Lev (1962). *Thought and Language*. Cambridge, MA: MIT Press.

Walker, C. B. F. (1987). *Cuneiform*. Berkeley: University of California Press.

Warschauer, Mark (2000). "Language, Identity and the Internet." In B. Kolko, L. Nakamura and G. Rodman (eds.), *Race in Cyberspace*, 151–70. New York: Routledge.

Wingo, E. Otha (1972). *Latin Punctuation in the Classical Age*. The Hague: Mouton.

Xu, Bing (2014). *Book from the Ground: From Point to Point*. Cambridge, MA: MIT Press.

Yuasa, Masahide, Saito, Keiichi, and Mukawa, Naoki (2011). "Brain Activity When Reading Sentences and Emoticons: An fMRI Study of Verbal and Nonverbal Communication." *Electronics and Communications in Japan* 94: 17–24.

Zantides, Evripides (ed.) (2014). *Semiotics and Visual Communication: Concepts and Practices*. Cambridge: Cambridge Scholars Publishing.

INDEX